Historic Australian Churches 1

A MISSION TO EVANGELISE

The Heidelberg Mission and St John the Evangelist

Kevin Andrews

A MISSION TO EVANGELISE

The Heidelberg Mission and St John the Evangelist

Kevin Andrews

Connor Court Publishing

Published in 2024 by Connor Court Publishing Pty Ltd

Copyright © Kevin Andrews 2024

All rights reserved. No part of this book may be reproduced or transmitted in any form or by any means, electronic or mechanical, including photo copying, recording or by any information storage and retrieval system, without prior permission in writing from the publisher.

Connor Court Publishing Pty Ltd
PO Box 7257
Redland Bay QLD 4165
sales@connorcourt.com
www.connorcourt.com
Phone 0497-900-685

Printed in Australia

ISBN: 9781922324490

Front cover design: Maria Giordano

Front cover picture: St John the Evangelist archives.

To the faithful parishioners of the Heidelberg Mission and the parish of St John the Evangelist, Heidelberg.

The moment has come to commit all of the Church's energies to the new evangelisation ... No believer in Christ, no institution of the Church can avoid this supreme duty: to proclaim Christ to all peoples.

- Pope John Paul II, *Redemptoris Missio*, December 1990

Contents

Foreword 11
1. Catholicism in Australia 13
2. A New Settlement 21
3. The Heidelberg Mission and Mary MacKillop 27
4. Establishing a Parish 31
5. An Expanding Mission 39
6. Towards Federation 45
7. A New Century 53
8. The Sisters of Mercy and Daniel Mannix 59
9. Expanding Catholic Education 65
10. Depression and War 71
11. Post-war Expansion 77
12. Social Upheaval and Liturgical Change 83
13. The End of the Irish Era 89
14. The Impact of John Paul II 93
15. Renovations and Celebrations 99
16. The 21st Century 105
17. A Mission to Evangelise 113
Appendix – Priests at Heidelberg 117
Select Bibliography 119

Foreword

Christianity has been present in Australia from the days of the first fleet. It was on the ships of the French explorer Lapérouse, who arrived at Botany Bay just six days after Captain Arthur Philip, that the first Catholic Masses were celebrated in the new colony.

The first census in 1836 of the region we now know as Victoria, revealed fourteen Catholics in the small village on the Yarra, who were meeting to say the Rosary in a cottage. Within three years a temporary Catholic Church had been built, being replaced by the original St Francis church in 1841. As Melbourne expanded, the Church established 'Missions' in the outlying rural areas of the new settlement, first at Coburg and then at Heidelberg in 1848.

This book continues this remarkable story and picks up the particular history of the Heidelberg Mission and its first Parish, St John the Evangelist. From this humble beginning sprang the network of Catholic Churches and parishes throughout what is now the eastern half of metropolitan Melbourne.

The Heidelberg Mission and the parish of St John the Evangelist is a fitting subject for the first monograph in a series about historic Australian churches.

Kevin Andrews reminds us of the commitment and sacrifices of generations of faithful Christians who constructed churches, established schools, sponsored services, and built the vibrant communities that have contributed to a prosperous nation founded on a recognition of the inherent dignity and liberty of the individual.

For almost two centuries, priests and parishioners at Heidelberg — and throughout the eastern and north-eastern areas of Melbourne — have engaged in a mission to evangelise, which continues today. Set against changing eras, this book tells the ongoing story of their challenges and achievements, of human lives and notably the strength and endurance of families. It is an inspiration for us to continue their work of sharing the Gospel of Jesus Christ.

Most Rev Peter A Comensoli

Archbishop of Melbourne

1

Catholicism in Australia

The first known Catholic contact with the land now known as Australia was by the Spanish explorer, Pedro Fernandez de Quiros who landed in the New Hebrides in 1606. Believing it to be the fabled great southern continent, he named it *Australis del Espiritu Sancto* — the Southern Land of the Holy Spirit. His deputy, Luis Vaz de Torres sailed through the strait separating Australia from Papua New Guinea later the same year.

The name 'Australia' — meaning southern land — had been used from Roman times; and the dedication to the Holy Spirit for many centuries. The explorer, Matthew Flinders popularised it in the early 1800s and it was adopted by the British Admiralty in 1824.

The first permanent Catholic presence was part of the British settlement in 1788. Although Catholics constituted about ten per cent of the convicts sentenced to transportation to Australia — of which more than half were Irish — there were no Catholic priests in the new colony for the first decade after Captain Arthur Phillip landed at Sydney Cove. The first Masses on the continent were celebrated on the *Boussole* and *L'Astolabe*, the ships on which the French explorer Jean-François de Galaup, comte de Lapérouse, arrived in Botany Bay just six days after Captain Arthur Phillip's First Fleet in 1788. The first Catholic burial was of the Franciscan friar and astronomer, Claude-François Louis Receveur who died — of injuries sustained in a conflict with the locals on the Samoan Islands — while the French ships were in Botany Bay.

Other Christian denominations didn't have much of a presence in the first decade after settlement either. The Rev Richard Johnson was recruited by William Wilberforce as chaplain to the First Fleet and Church of England clergyman to the new colony. Writing in 1792, he expressed his frustration of being the only pastor in the colony: "The colony already begins to spread, and will probably spread more and more every year, both by new settlements formed in different places under the crown, and by a number of individuals continually becoming settlers. Thus, the extent of what I call my parish, and consequently of my parochial duty, is enlarging daily."

The expanse of the colony was to grow exponentially after Gregory Blaxland, William Charles Wentworth and William Lawson successfully crossed the Blue Mountains in 1813, opening up the vast inland plains of New South Wales.

Johnson was replaced by Samuel Marsden in 1794. Subsequently a missionary to New Zealand, Marsden occupied both religious and secular posts, the latter a magistrate as well as a wealthy farmer. His attitude to the Irish convicts hardly engendered mutual respect. Writing in *The Fatal Shore*, Robert Hughes cites a memorandum authored by Marsden: "No Confidence whatever can be placed in them... [If Catholicism in Australia] were tolerated they would assemble together from every Quarter, not so much from a desire of celebrating Mass, as to recite the Miseries and Injustice of their Banishment, the Hardships they suffer, and to inflame one another's minds with some wild Scheme of Revenge."

Presbyterian Christianity came to Australia with the arrival of members from a number of Presbyterian denominations in Great Britain at the end of the 18th century. The first known Presbyterian to arrive in the colony was John Hunter, the captain of the *HMS Sirius* in the First Fleet. He had been a Church of Scotland minister before his naval career. The first Methodist minister to arrive in the colony was Samuel Leigh in 1815.

The first priests

In 1800, three Irish priests, James Harold, James Dixon and Peter O'Neill, were amongst the convicts who arrived in Sydney, having been convicted of 'complicity' in the 1798 Irish Rebellion. One of them, Fr James Dixon was conditionally emancipated in 1803, and permitted to celebrate Mass and minister to Catholics, including convicts and some members of the marines, until his permission was revoked following the Castle Hill Rebellion in 1804. Although he had pleaded with the rebels to cease, his facilities were withdrawn by the governor. Another priest, the Irish Cistercian monk, Fr Jeremiah O'Flynn subsequently travelled to New South Wales after being made a Prefect Apostolic of New Holland. He secretly performed his priestly duties until discovered, arrested and deported to London. Fr Dixon also returned although it appears that he ministered privately until departing NSW in 1809.

Following outcry in Britain about the absence of priests in the colony, two priests, Fr John Joseph Therry and Fr Philip Connolly, were permitted to travel to Australia in 1820 to minister to Catholics. Lachlan Macquarie, perhaps the most impressive of the early governors, was not only a skilled administrator, but a humane man steeped in Christianity. Although he had earlier believed that religious uniformity was better for public order, he accepted the decision of the government in London that Catholic priests be sent to the colony and officially recognised, including payment of a salary. Welcoming, he remained cautious, instructing them that they were permitted to marry Roman Catholics only and must not proselytise. Father Therry treated the Governor's 'instructions' as loose guidelines to be ignored when pastoral necessity demanded it. A year later, Governor Lachlan Macquarie laid the foundation stone for the first St Mary's church in Sydney.

While Connolly subsequently moved to Van Diemen's Land, Therry remained in New South Wales, staying in the colony for 44 years. For five years, he was the only priest in NSW, travelling vast distances throughout the colony to minister to his flock. For decades, there were very few or no priests available for the growing number of Catholics in the new colonies. Despite this impediment, the faith was nurtured in homes across the settlement, in particular through a devotion to Our Lady and the Rosary.

Speaking in 1988, Edward Clancy, the Cardinal Archbishop of Sydney, observed that "it seems that the great pioneering priest, John Joseph Therry, intended that this Mother Church of Australia should be dedicated to Our Lady, Help of Christians." The three bishops in Australia, together with their 15 pioneer priests, petitioned Rome after their Australasian synod in 1844 for the recognition of Our Lady Help of Christians as the patroness of Australia. Formal approbation arrived in 1852. The title had a long history, having origins in at least the third century and usage over subsequent eras.

The English Benedictines

The ongoing troubles in Ireland and the legal impediments for Catholics in the UK meant that the early priests in the colony were French and English, despite the presence of a growing number of Irish Catholics. As a consequence, the English Benedictines were favoured by the authorities in London to journey to New South Wales.

The hierarchy in Australia was established by Pope Gregory XVI in 1834 upon the urging of Fr Bernard Ullathorne. Originally, it was part of the diocese of Mauritius. Ullathorne visited Australia between 1833 and 1836 as Vicar-General to the Bishop of Mauritius, William Morris. The separation of Australia from Mauritius resulted in the appointment of Fr John Bede Polding OSB as the Vicar Apostolic of New Holland, Van Diemen's Land and the adjoining islands in 1834. He arrived in Hobart in August 1835. While there, he blessed the foundation stone of Australia's oldest, extant Catholic Church, St John the Evangelist at Richmond, 16 miles (27 kilometres) north east of Hobart. A month after docking in Hobart, Polding left a priest to assist the ministry to Catholics in Van Diemen's Land before sailing to his final destination, Sydney. In 1842, Polding was appointed the first bishop, and then archbishop, of Sydney. He served in the role for 32 years, retiring in 1874, dying three years later at the age of 82.

Polding was respected by the colonial authorities for his positive influence on the convicts. It was arranged for him to meet arriving ships and speak to the new convicts, although many of the Irish remained suspicious of the English Benedictines because of the ongoing antipathy between the two countries.

The archbishop began the task of building churches, schools and other educational institutions such St John's College at the University of Sydney. He introduced the Sisters of Charity and the Christian Brothers to Australia and established a new Australian congregation, the Sisters of the Good Samaritan. Archbishop Polding travelled widely throughout the colony. He acceded to the request of Catholics in Melbourne for a priest in 1838; and on his journey to Rome in 1846, gained approval for the creation of a new diocese centred on Melbourne in the Port Phillip District.

From the outset, the church in Australia was on a mission to evangelise.

Archbishop Goold (above) and the oldest extant Catholic Church in Australia St John the Evangelist at Richmond Tasmania (St. John's archives; The author)

2

A New Settlement

The first European settlement of Melbourne occurred in 1835, when John Batman and John Faulkner separately established settlements on the Yarra River, having crossed Bass Strait from Van Diemen's Land, now Tasmania. They had made treaties with the local indigenous tribe, the Wurundjeri, who had lived in the area for thousands of years. These agreements were annulled by the Governor of NSW, Richard Bourke, in 1837. The region was declared the Port Phillip District of New South Wales, and the new settlement named 'Melbourne' the following year after the then prime minister of the United Kingdom, William Lamb, the 2nd Viscount Melbourne. Settlers arrived from both Van Diemen's Land and overland from New South Wales.

The Christian denominations established themselves from the earliest years of the new settlement. A Church of England bishop, Charles Perry was appointed in 1846 and consecrated at Westminster Abbey the following year. With the appointment of a bishop, Melbourne was declared a city, just five days before Queen Victoria's 63-year-reign began.

In 1839, a small group of Catholics gathered in Melbourne with the object of building a church and securing a priest for the settlement. The small Catholic community petitioned John Bede Polding, the first Archbishop of Sydney. They also raised the impressive sum of £120 towards establishing a church. Bishop Polding responded to the request by sending a Franciscan, Fr Patrick Bonaventure Geoghegan, who had been born in Dublin and educated in Ireland and Portugal before travelling to Australia in 1838.

Described as "a round, chubby, natty little man, a perfect picture of health and cheerfulness," Fr Geoghegan was known as a distinguished preacher.

There are reports of a "temporary timber chapel … built alongside of the home of Monsieur Bodecin" a French carpenter who lived at Collins Street West. Interestingly, the French influence in the early days of Melbourne was notable. The first Mass was celebrated in a partly built store on the corner of Elizabeth and Little Collins Street. Coming from Europe — predominantly England, Ireland and Scotland, where grand churches had been built for centuries — the experience of the new settlers was stark. The first Mass centre in Melbourne had a wooden chest mounted on a table, as the altar. It was decorated by Mrs Jeremiah Coffey, the first Catholic teacher in the settlement.

St Francis Church

A small timber chapel was constructed in 1839 on the site of what is now St Francis church on Lonsdale Street. The current building, which has been modified and expanded over the decades, was commenced in 1841 and opened in 1846 as Melbourne's first Catholic cathedral. The initial population of just 177 in 1836 began to grow rapidly as more people moved to Melbourne. By 1839, there were an estimated 500 Catholics in Melbourne. At the time of the opening of the first St Francis church, the Catholic population of Melbourne was just over 1,000 people. There were just 6 priests, based at St Francis, in 1850. They were described as "young priests, fresh out of college, without experience." It was on this foundation that the Catholic church in Victoria was established.

Two years later, Melbourne's first Catholic bishop, James Alipius Goold arrived. The first Catholic secondary school was established at St Francis. It became St Patrick's when it moved to Victoria Parade, East Melbourne in 1853. The Christian Brothers arrived in 1868, establishing a college in Victoria Parade.

As a consequence of the growing population, the small settlement began to expand, with houses and farms being established in the adjacent areas. The first land sales were held in 1838 at Keelbundoora, an aboriginal name since shortened to Bundoora on the east bank of the Darebin Creek. The area to the west of the creek was named Jika Jika. The land was used primarily for sheep grazing and grain production. It was originally part of the lands of the Wurundjeri people. Local land owners established the Heidelberg Road Trust in 1841, the first Local Government body in the Port Philip District. Three decades later, the Shire of Heidelberg was created. It extended from Fairfield to Hurstbridge.

The new settlement continued to grow in the late 1840s, with farms being established along the Darebin Creek and the Yarra River to meet the demand for food. By 1851, the Melbourne settlement had grown to some 23,000 people.

Just three years after Melbourne's settlement, allotments of land at Warringal — an aboriginal name for Eagle's Nest — were sold. Located on the Yarra River some seven miles (11 kilometres) northeast of the new city, the allotments were quickly settled with houses and shops that serviced the growing farming communities in the area. Among the buildings in this new rural outpost were the Olde England Hotel (1848) and St John's Church of England (1851).

Two months after his arrival from Sydney, Bishop Goold wrote to the Superintendent of the Port Phillip District, Charles La Trobe requesting two acres of land to build a Catholic church, school and dwelling at Warringal, by then re-named Heidelberg. The original grant of land was on the east side of Cape Street, where Our Lady of Mercy College now stands. A second, successful application moved it to where a church was erected on the west side of the street.

The Heidelberg Mission and St John the Evangelist

In that year, 1848, the Heidelberg Mission was established to serve the needs of the growing Catholic population of the region.

St Monica's School (The Author)

3

The Heidelberg Mission

The first Catholic services were celebrated in the Heidelberg region in May 1848, in the homes of Alexander MacKillop and Michael Pender, two of the local farmers. Present at the Mass in the home of MacKillop and his wife, Flora MacDonald was their six-year-old daughter, Marie Ellen, known to us as Mother Mary MacKillop and subsequently St Mary of the Cross MacKillop.

Later that year, Bishop Goold requested land for the church and established the Heidelberg Mission, the forerunner of the parish of St John the Evangelist. The Heidelberg Mission covered a vast tract of what is now eastern Melbourne. It spread north to Whittlesea, east to Healesville and Warburton and south to Brighton. Farms interspersed uninhabited lands. Small villages were established in various places across the region.

The first priority for the Heidelberg Catholics was the

establishment of a school. The need for a school was recognised by July 1848 when a report to the Denominational Schools Board noted that "there were sufficient Catholic Children to entitle a teacher to Government aid." As Bishop Goold observed the following March, "the school could not be undertaken without aid." At the time, churches and schools received government support in proportion to the amount subscribed by the students attending and the numbers.

Opened in 1850, it was a primitive structure, constructed from roughly sawn wooden panels with no windows, measuring just 30 feet by 15 feet (9 metres by 4.5 metres). Although it had a fireplace, it was described as "wretched in winter." The government school inspector described it as "altogether a most miserable affair – quite unworthy of government aid." There were 26 pupils each paying sixpence a week, although a private Catholic school was also operating in the vicinity with 15 pupils, and another at Boroondara with 37 students. The school, which had cost £35, was used for the first religious services. It was soon replaced by a simple wooden building, dedicated to St Francis Xavier.

The French writer, photographer and adventurer, Antoine Fauchery recorded his visit to the Mission in 1851. Searching for the church, he eventually noticed a belfry: "I espied a little bell installed in a forked tree whose top had been lopped." Fauchery described the small church nearby: "A long hut made of planks barely planed or not planed at all, and surmounted by a wooden cross."

Peering through a crack in the planks, he observed "the most modest altar that you would be able to find among the most modest of our little Corpus Christi Chapels; a sort of big packing-case covered with a white cloth, a box-wood crucifix, and image, flowers and two copper candlesticks flitted out with their candles."

A new church

The local Catholic community — aware that their rough wooden structure was inadequate for a growing population — turned their minds to a more permanent church. The *Melbourne Herald* reported that on Easter Monday 1851, Bishop Goold laid the foundation stone for a new church, dedicated to St Monica. When formally proclaimed a parish in 1851, Heidelberg became the third parish to be established in the archdiocese, the earlier two being St Francis Melbourne and St Paul's Coburg.

A feature of the era — repeated over the coming decades — was the support from other denominations for the construction of the church. Cooperation with other denominations was common in the era. At the blessing of the new church, recognition was given to the assistance that "the Catholic people" had received from "their Protestant brethren in gathering funds for the church and also on the purchase of the sounding bell."

The first resident priest of the Heidelberg Mission, Fr Viventius Bourgeois was appointed in 1851. After arriving in Australia in

1843 with three other French priests, Fr Bourgeois served as a theologian to Bishop Polding in Sydney before being posted to Bathurst and subsequently Melbourne.

Antoine Fauchery described him in his *Letters from a Miner in Australia*: "In the middle of the room, furnished on both sides with wretched wooden benches, a man of about forty, with a respectable corpulency, bareheaded and clad in the long black Cassock worn by ecclesiastics, was humbly keeling on the floor, not in prayerful meditation, but vigorously sweeping ... under the seats, which were fastened to the floor... from time to time, he stopped out of breath, drew from his pocket a wipe handkerchief which he mopped his sweat-drenched brow ... and gave a few deep sighs."

The French author and traveller described a pleasant afternoon with Fr Bourgeois in the modest two-room presbytery with just two chairs, a sofa bed and a table: "I spent a whole day with this most excellent abbe ... the most affable Frenchman, the most amiable talker, the most indulgent confessor that I have ever met in my life. He gave me information, advice, encouragement, and moreover, he did not talk to me about Hell ..." The two met on other occasions, the first priest giving "the measure of Australia as it was" and expressing every confidence in the future of the country.

Fr Bourgeois remained at Heidelberg until Easter 1857. Having spent 14 years in Australia, he returned to Europe.

4

Establishing a Parish

The year 1851 was significant for the Catholics of Heidelberg: the school opened, construction of a permanent church was commenced and the first priest was appointed to the Heidelberg Mission.

It was also an important year for Melbourne: The Port Phillip District was declared the new Colony of Victoria, and gold was discovered. Coming just sixteen years after the settlement of Melbourne, the colonial status reflected the rapid growth of the region.

Charles La Trobe was appointed the inaugural Governor. A deeply religious man, whose father and grandfather were friends of John Newton and William Wilberforce, La Trobe opposed slavery and supported the establishment of religious, cultural and educational institutions in the new colony. Generous land grants were made to religious denominations for the construction of schools and churches. "It is not by individual aggrandisement, by the possession of numerous flocks or herds, or by costly acres, that the people shall secure for the country enduring prosperity and happiness, but by the acquisition and maintenance of sound religious and moral institutions without which no country can become truly great," observed La Trobe.

In the 1850s, Heidelberg was a small rural settlement amidst surrounding farms. To the east, Major Charles Newman established an extensive cattle-run along the Yarra River extending from Templestowe to East Doncaster. Further east, James Anderson also farmed cattle on his large property closer to Warrandyte.

It was at Anderson's Creek that gold was first discovered in Victoria in late June 1851, attracting hundreds of prospectors to the area. Much larger discoveries at Ballarat and Clunes soon attracted thousands of adventurers away from Melbourne to the new gold fields. It was the beginning of a boom period for Melbourne and Victoria. Immigrants flooded into the colony to experience a standard of living surpassing their previous experiences in Europe and elsewhere. The population of Melbourne doubled in one year alone between 1853 and 1854. For many who had fled the great Irish famine (1845-52), Victoria was a nirvana that they could only have imagined in their wildest dreams.

Even as the parishioners of Heidelberg were building their second church, St Monica's, they were contemplating a larger building to meet the needs of a growing parish. St Monica's was originally planned as a brick church, but was never completed. Instead, a wooden church dedicated to the mother of St Augustine was used, to be replaced by the church dedicated to St John the Evangelist in 1861.

Presbytery

The first priest at the Heidelberg Mission, Fr Bourgeois initially resided at Preston, about a mile and a half west of Heidelberg near the Darebin Creek. By the time Antione Fauchery first visited him in 1853, the priest was domiciled in a small two-room hut adjacent to the first church. An advertisement in *The Argus* invited tenders for "a rubble stone cottage with a kitchen attached" in September 1854, the building being the new presbytery. The following year, a rubble stone presbytery had been constructed at a cost of £400 comprising funds from the government and donations from parishioners.

In 1857, the second priest to serve the Heidelberg Mission, Fr Gerald Ward was appointed. Born in County Cork, Ireland in 1806, he undertook his seminary studies and early ministry in England before volunteering to serve in Australia, arriving in 1850. Fr Ward was the first priest at Williamstown and secretary to the bishop before his appointment to Heidelberg. He was engaged in evangelisation, establishing an orphanage in Prahran, as well as the first Australian branch of the Society of St Vincent de Paul. He also founded a circulating library at Heidelberg.

Fr Ward was described as "a short, stout priest of about 45" when he arrived from the English Mission in Cheshire and Lancashire. A report of the time stated that he "seemed unfitted to undertake the pioneering work of a new diocese" where he "shared the labours and hardships in the early priests." *The Advocate* subsequently described him as "an exceedingly nervous man" and a "pious, zealous and an unostentatious priest . . . noted for his benevolence and practical charity. . ."

Although he was born in Tipperary, Fr Ward had the distinction of being the first priest ordained in Victoria, having emigrated with his parents as a small boy in 1841. He was described as "a fine stamp of a man" noted for "giving parties for the children of the parish." His brother, Edward, wrote the *Chronicles of Early Melbourne* under the pseudonym, Garryowen. In frail health, Fr Ward died just nine months after his appointment to Heidelberg.

He was replaced by Fr. John Hoyne, who was born in County Kilkenny and educated at the famed All Hallows College, Dublin, before serving as a professor of mathematics at the college of Calcutta, India for six years. When the diocese of Calcutta was transferred to the Society of Jesus, Fr Hoyne came to Melbourne, serving at St Francis parish for eight months before his appointment to Heidelberg in January 1858. Soon after his arrival, Fr Hoyne sought permission to construct a new church to replace St Monica's.

Records compiled by Fr Hoyne indicate that there was an average attendance of 200 parishioners at Heidelberg, with 60 monthly communicants. There were 6 marriages and 54 baptisms in the first five months of 1858. The average attendance at the school was 42 pupils.

A year after the opening of the first stage of the newly constructed church of St John the Evangelist, Fr Hoyne was transferred to Geelong West. He later served in the Ballarat diocese at Warrnambool and Hamilton before being appointed Vicar General in Ballarat. His last years were spent as the chaplain to the Good Shepherd Sisters in Hobart. Before departing Heidelberg, he paid off the remaining debt on the new church from his own savings.

St John the Evangelist

In 1859, the Dean of St Francis, Fr Dean Fitzpatrick laid the foundation stone for the third church, a bluestone building designed by the renowned colonial architect, William Wardell. A previous attempt to lay the foundation stone by the Bishop of Hobart, Dr Robert Wilson in July 1858 was abandoned because of a violent storm.

The parish was known as St Monica's for a decade from 1851. Marriages and christenings were registered as at St Monica's.

William Wardell designed some of the most important colonial buildings of the era, including St Patrick's Cathedral, Melbourne; St Mary's Cathedral, Sydney; and Victoria's Government House. He also designed 14 parish churches in Melbourne, including the church dedicated to St John the Evangelist at Heidelberg.

Born in London in 1823, Wardell studied under the noted Gothic architect Augustus Pugin, designing a number of churches in England and Scotland. In 1843, he converted to Catholicism, and immigrated to Australia in 1858 to take up the position of Government Architect in the City of Melbourne. He subsequently moved to Sydney in 1878, while still overseeing the construction of buildings in Melbourne, especially St Patrick's Cathedral, which was not consecrated until 1897.

When opened, Wardell's church at Heidelberg was smaller than the present structure, comprising the sanctuary, the side room (chapel), sacristy and three bays of the current nave. It wasn't until 1909, some 48 years later, that extensions were added to complete the original design.

The church was constructed from blue stone in the gothic design favoured by Wardell, with great interlocking beams of Swedish red deal timber supporting the roof. Two Celtic crosses surmounted the steep slate roof. There was a temporary porch. The new building was a simpler but similar design to St Mary's East St Kilda.

A chimney and fireplace were incorporated into the side room, now the St Mary of the Cross MacKillop chapel. The external door to the room was added later. The room was used initially for the administration of the parish, as well as a meeting room for parishioners. It was later utilised by the Sisters of Mercy as a chapel.

On Sunday, 14th April 1861, the church of St John the Evangelist was blessed and opened by Dr Quinn, the newly appointed Bishop of Queensland. Reporting on the opening, the *Hamilton Spectator* observed that "the church is beautifully situated commanding a splendid view of the Plenty Ranges." The cost of building the church in 1861 was £4000 pounds, the equivalent of the lifetime earnings of a labourer of the era.

The population of Melbourne had expanded to some 37,000 people by 1861. In November that year, some 4,000 of the inhabitants journeyed to Flemington to watch the racehorse *Archer* win the first Melbourne Cup. A few years earlier, in August 1858, teams from Scotch College and Melbourne Grammar School played the first game of what would become Australian rules football, designed to keep cricket players fit during winter.

Two years after the establishment of the Heidelberg Parish in 1851, others were created at Brighton, Williamstown and Richmond. Soon after, the number extended to Keilor and South Melbourne to service the growing population. A church was also built in West Melbourne in 1854. By 1860, work had commenced on the construction of St Patrick's Cathedral.

It was not until 1874 that the rural dioceses of Ballarat and

Sandhurst (Bendigo) were created. A decade later, Gippsland was excised from Melbourne with the creation of the Diocese of Sale in 1887.

From the very outset of the Heidelberg Mission, raising the funds necessary to build new churches and schools was an ongoing imperative. The parish was rarely free of debt, often borrowing more funds while paying down existing liabilities. While a mostly middle-class area now, it wasn't always the case. There were some wealthy farmers and landowners, but many people living in the rural area in the 19th century were labourers. The first Parish Priest, Fr Bourgeois, reported that the Catholics "there were not rich and their means were very limited." Another report noted that the Catholics of the era were principally from the labouring classes.

5

An Expanding Mission

Fr. William Finn was appointed the fourth parish priest in 1862, a position he occupied for the following 15 years. Born in Tipperary, Ireland, he had emigrated to Australia as a child with his parents in 1841. Educated at St Patrick's College, East Melbourne, Fr Finn was one of first students of the University of Melbourne. As priest to the Heidelberg Mission, his task was to service the Catholic families in the vast rural area east of the city. Another description of Heidelberg in 1862 described it as "a tiny village with a sprinkling of not too affluent Catholics in the neighbourhood."

> The mission was ... developing rapidly, tiny settlements springing up in all directions. The Upper Yarra district was then a mining, pastoral and agricultural area. Mining was being carried on at Diamond Creek, Warburton and other places, while isolated parties of diggers were fossicking for gold along the upper reaches of the Yarra Yarra. The rich river flats provided for the

grazing of large herds of cattle and land was being selected in ... the district, the fertile soil being capable of growing almost anything.

"There was much rich farmland around the tiny hamlets of Eltham and Healesville; and the Yan Yean waterworks" provided work for many Irish labourers "while in the hills around the village of Lilydale, a colony of Swiss vignerons were raising vines for a new wine industry." One of these families were the De Castellas. Hubert De Castella had a home and vineyard at Yering Station near Lilydale which was used as a Mass centre. They also had a residence 'Chartersville' in Ivanhoe, and supplied altar wine for the Mission. At one stage, the Ivanhoe home was leased to Walter Withers, one of the Heidelberg school artists.

Apart from the church at Heidelberg, there were no others in the region in the early years of the settlement. The resident priest would ride long distances, his Mass kit strapped to his saddle, to visit isolated farms and villages. Masses were conducted in houses such as the home of Captain John Sweeney at Eltham. Often staying overnight, the priest could travel from farm to farm, returning to Heidelberg days after departure. Fr Finn regularly visited the cattle stations at Yan Yean, Whittlesea, Hoddle's Creek, Linton, Healesville, St Andrew's diggings and Anderson's Creek.

Providing liturgical services and pastoring to the Catholics residing in the area covered by the Heidelberg Mission was an arduous task. The trek on horseback or by horse and buggy from Heidelberg to Healesville and return covered more than 60 miles (100 kilometres).

There were many places in the vast region where the priest stopped to celebrate Mass and attend to the other pastoral needs of his parishioners. Generally, Mass was celebrated in the outlying regions at least monthly.

When Fr Finn arrived in 1862, he faced the challenge of a scattered and growing Catholic population. Over the next 15 years, he embarked on an ambitious building program to establish Mass centres across the region. The original wooden church at Lilydale was replaced by a new granite building in 1870. A few months later, a small wooden church was constructed at Eltham. Other churches followed: at Diamond Creek in 1874, and Yan Yean subsequently.

The Catholics of the era may not have been wealthy, but they were generous. Apart from building churches, establishing schools for their children was a priority. Their generosity wasn't limited to local projects. Funds were raised for the Irish Famine Relief and for the assistance of persecuted priests in Germany.

The Bourke Church Act

In 1836, the *Church Act* was approved by the Colonial Office and passed by the NSW Legislative Council during the term of Governor Richard Bourke. The Act provided funding to the Catholic, Church of England and Presbyterian churches to employ clergy and erect churches. The amount for each denomination was determined by the number of their adherents.

The Act removed many of the privileges that the Church of England had enjoyed in NSW of which Victoria was then a part and placed Catholics and Anglicans on an equal basis. The Act was later to extend to the Methodists, which found some common ground with the Presbyterians in their opposition to the power of the Church of England.

The 1872 Education Act

In 1872 the Victorian Government passed the *Education Act* 1872, which had a significant impact on the provision of schooling in the state. The legislation set up the colony's public school system. It followed a Royal Commission into the subject. The Catholic Church had been the largest provider of schools in the colony prior to the changes and it opposed the proposals.

This new legislation made Victoria the first Australian colony to offer free, secular and compulsory education to its children. After 1872, rather than being controlled by religious and other private organisations, most schools were centrally controlled by the government education department.

Under the new Act children between the ages of six and fifteen had to attend school, and if they attended a government school their education was free. At the same time all government funding to religious schools stopped. Many religious schools chose to stop teaching religion and become a part of the new government system. But some — mostly all-Catholic schools — continued to run independently. Parents who chose to send their children to private religious schools had to pay school fees.

These changes added further burdens on Catholic families who had received government assistance with the education of their children. It would be almost a century before government assistance to them was again granted following a decision by the national government of Robert Menzies in the 1960s.

The changes didn't deter Catholics from building schools. In the region of the Heidelberg Mission, many more schools, both primary and secondary, were to be constructed over the coming decades.

The first Jesuit

The first member of the Society of Jesus to arrive in Australia was Fr Aloysius Kranewitter, who had been born at Innsbruck in the Austrian province of Tyrol in 1817. He emigrated to Australia with another Jesuit, Fr Maximilian Klinkowstroem, arriving in Adelaide in 1848. Fr Klinkowstroem returned to Europe in ill health soon after arriving. Fr Kranewitter moved to Sevenhill in the Clare Valley in 1848 where he planted vines and established the famous Jesuit winery. He expanded the settlement at Sevenhill until moving to Richmond in Melbourne in 1870.

His ministry was in the semi-rural districts of Nunawading and Heidelberg, Fr Kranewitter died at Heidelberg in 1880 and is buried at the Boroondara Cemetery, Kew.

St John the Evangelist 1861 with the Victorian premier in the centre; and the Presbytery c. 1880. (St John's archives)

6

Towards Federation

The last two decades of the 19th century saw the stirrings of change that would affect all Australians. Apart from Victoria, new colonies had been created in Tasmania (1825), Western Australia (1829), South Australia (1836) and Queensland (1859). By the 1880s there arose a movement to unite into one nation. The explorer, Matthew Flinders first used the description 'Australia' in 1804. From about 1817, the expression was in popular usage.

Friendly societies

There were no government payments for individuals and families experiencing unemployment, illness or adversity in the 19th century. It wasn't until after World War II that the welfare state became a reality.

Instead, Australians engaged with mutual support activities, most prominently the 'Friendly Societies' that flourished in the second half of the 1800s.

In these groups, working men pooled their money into a 'mutual fund' that they could use if they were sick, in distress or too old to work. The friendly societies often encouraged their members to engage with important moral and social issues.

The Australian Catholic Benefit Society, formed in Ballarat in 1868, was the largest Irish Catholic organisation in Australia. *The Argus* on April 21, 1896 reported that it had over 130 branches. It boasted some 41,000 members spread across almost 600 branches by 1920.

Despite discouragement by the bishops in 1888, Catholics also joined other groups. It would appear that the bishops were as concerned about the dilution of funds that may otherwise been directed to Catholic schools and services as any other issue, given that non-Catholics could join the ACBS.

While these organisations concentrated on the material welfare of their members, some expanded their activities. The most prominent of these groups was the Australian Natives Association. Established in 1871, the ANA became the most influential organisation in colonial Australia. It had 129 branches in Victoria alone by the end of the 19th century, covering the whole colony, including the region of the Heidelberg Mission. By 1910 it had 28,844 members from all types of jobs and social classes.

The ANA campaigned for making 26th January 'Australia Day'. It used its journal, *Advance Australia*, to argue for minimum wages, votes for women and free, non-religious education. Prominent amongst its members were prime ministers Edmund Barton, Alfred Deakin, James Scullin and Francis Forde, the latter two being Catholics. It was a key organisation in advocating federation.

Unlike the Australian Catholic Benefit Society, which rejected a motion in support of federation because it was a political issue, the ANA was prominent in public affairs. In 1884, the ANA threw its support behind the federation of the colonies.

Of all the colonists, Victorians — along with Tasmanians — were strongly in favour of federation, while the results in the largest colony, NSW was much closer. The labour movement was also more sceptical about the proposal.

New schools and churches

While there was considerable attention given to the direction of Australia, there was much to do locally. A new Catholic Common School — dedicated to St Monica, the mother of St Augustine — had been opened in Heidelberg in 1871. *The Advocate* reported that "this latter addition to our public schools will accommodate 150 children. It has cost £600. When it is stated that the Board of Education has absolutely refused to aid it because it is a non-vested one, the difficulty of completing such a structure in a district where Catholics are in a great minority will be understood. It is really too bad that Catholics should be thus treated by the Board all over Victoria, whilst upon every principle of justice and fair play, they are entitled when building schools to a quota towards the building fund."

New stables, which continue to stand adjacent to the presbytery, were also constructed; and work began on a new church at Diamond Creek. The presbytery was reconstructed and enlarged at a cost of £1,700 in 1875, taking its current form.

Four decades after its settlement, Heidelberg had changed little. It was described in the 1880s as "a remote, sleepy (village) . . . with its winding country roads, its wooded hills and its quiet village life." In 1889, both reticulated water and gas was connected to the Heidelberg Village, but it would be another three decades before the village was incorporated in the metropolitan sewerage system.

The mission to evangelise continued apace, with new churches at Diamond Creek (1874), Yan Yean (1879), Yarra Glen (1887), Healesville (1888) Lilydale (1889) and Whittlesea (1896). A largely forgotten feature of the 1800s was the cooperation between Christian congregations to construct churches. At Warrandyte, for example, members of the various denominations contributed to the construction of St Stephen's Church of England. This cooperation continued with efforts to build the Catholic Church. The church at Yarra Glen, built some two decades later, was constructed on an acre of land donated by a member of the Presbyterian church.

Lilydale became a new mission centre in 1889, relieving some of the burden on the priests from Heidelberg. To the north, Whittlesea remained a part of the Heidelberg Mission until 1910. Two priests, Fr John Horan (1879-1882) and Fr Dennis O'Callaghan (1882-1907), carried the burden of the era, the latter for a record 25 years. Each man had been born in Ireland and trained at All Hallows College, Dublin. After departing Heidelberg, Fr Horan eventually moved to America. Fr O'Callaghan was described in *The Advocate* as a "great favourite with members of other denominations as with those of his own fold ... owing to his genial disposition ... integrity and principles." He was "a most devoted and attentive clergyman ... most sociable to all those with whom he came in contact."

In his first four years at the parish, Fr O'Callaghan raised £2,700 and paid off the debt. He also built churches at Eltham, Diamond Creek, Healesville and Whittlesea, enlarged the church at Yan Yean and constructed a new church at Yarra Glen. There were constant fundraising activities to support these activities. Fr O'Callaghan's health declined, in part a consequence of the gruelling regimen. On the Sundays that he celebrated Mass at Healesville, he would fast from midnight, ride the 30 miles to celebrate 7.00 am service before returning to Heidelberg for the 11.00 am Eucharist. He retired in 1907 following a year's sick leave, dying in 1911. He was interned at the Warringal Cemetery, the only parish priest to be buried locally.

The first assistant priest, Fr Joseph Sheehy was appointed in 1877, having moved from Hobart. Another of the early assistant priests, Fr Hugh McKenna was appointed to ease the considerable burden on the Mission in 1884, but died at the age of just 29 after celebrating Mass at Lilydale in January 1885.

In 1886, Melbourne's first archbishop, James Alipius Goold died. An obituary by Francis Quinlan, a judge of the Victorian County Court (1882-91) — who had emigrated from Ireland in search of gold and later studied law at the University of Melbourne – captured the enormity of the archbishop's contributions to church and colony:

> He was a bishop whose duties can never be equalled, by reason of their inseparable association with the circumstances of the early days. The whole face of the colony is now changed that it is impossible for any of his successors to labour in his footsteps. The reason is this: he came at a time that was most exciting in the history of this colony when people were pouring in at a rate of a thousand a week. He had to supervise a territory of enormous extent, teeming with human souls that wanted saving, and with children that wanted education. It was a task for a Hercules, but he did it. I remember his excursions through the bush in the olden times. He was obliged to do all his travelling on horseback, and he did it. How unostentatious he was! How zealous! How indefatigable! How under his mild bland exterior he carried the heart of a Christian warrior! I remember his coming to Ballarat at the time of the Eureka riots, and I know that for a fact that his presence and influence there had more effect in upholding law and order than all the soldiers and police put together… I have a vivid recollection of the kindness and courtesy with which he was treated by the English officers in the camp, and in their anxiety that the Bishop would stay with them, but his Lordship politely but firmly declined their kind invitation, remarking, 'I must go to

my own people.' And he went to his own people, and slept that night amongst them in a little tent. On the following morning I was present when he spoke. A more unobtrusive orator I never heard, and yet I do not think I ever heard one more effectual. I was assured by the officers and others that Dr Goold's advice and exhortation to the people effected a revolution for the good, and they personally expressed their gratitude to him for his timely visit and his tranquilising words.

A year after his death, Archbishop Goold was succeeded by Thomas Joseph Carr in the Melbourne See. Born and educated in Ireland, he had been bishop of Galway before his appointment to Melbourne.

The last two decades of the 19th century was a difficult time economically for the colony. A property boom of the 1880s led to a depression the following decade, with real GDP falling by 17 per cent between 1892 and 1893. The expansion of the nation's major industry, wool growing, into more arid areas also contributed to economic weakness. A significant portion of the Australian banking system collapsed, resulting in a more severe impact than the 'Great Depression' of the 1930s.

Despite the economic challenges, the belief that Australians were 'one people [with] one destiny' to adopt the expression of the father of federation, Henry Parkes gained increasing support. The idea of being an Australian was reflected in other spheres of national life. The song 'Advance Australia Fair', to become the national anthem a century later, was penned in 1876.

Closer to home, the Australian landscape was depicted in a new manner by Arthur Streeton, Walter Withers, Tom Roberts, Frederick McCubbin and others. Many of their works were painted around Heidelberg, giving the *plein air* movement its name, the Heidelberg School. Arthur Streeton's 1889 painting, *Golden Summer, Eaglemont*, depicts sheep grazing on dry slopes of Mount Eagle, with the Yarra Valley below and the Dandenong Ranges in the distance. Other paintings of the era, including David Davies' *Moonrise over Templestowe* also illustrate the rural landscape of the area in the late 1800s.

7

A New Century

A new century brought renewed optimism to the residents of Heidelberg. The financial constraints of the 1890s were lifting and hope in the future growing. The 20th century heralded a new nation with the creation of the Commonwealth of Australia in 1901 and the former colonies becoming states.

The opening of the railway line from Melbourne to Heidelberg in 1888 boosted the prosperity of the growing village situated in the midst of a rich farming region. The first cars appeared on Australian roads in the late 1890s. By 1925, when the popular T-model Ford was introduced locally, the numbers continued to increase. The steep Burgundy Street in Heidelberg became a favoured location for hill climbs, a popular form of motorsports during the era, with the first Automobile Club of Victoria event conducted in March in 1904. Finely dressed crowds lined the sides of the steep road to cheer on the competitors. One of the most prominent drivers was Sir Reginald Talbot, the Governor of Victoria.

The Heidelberg village and surrounding farms had relied on a road from Fitzroy to transport people and goods for many decades. The road generally followed what is now Heidelberg Road. The population of the Shire of Heidelberg — covering some 41 square miles — had grown from 4,413 people living in 716 dwellings in 1891 to 5,008 people living in 817 dwellings in 1901.

With about a quarter of the local population Catholic, the church and school were becoming inadequate for the growing demand. The new Archbishop of Melbourne, Thomas Joseph Carr, visited Heidelberg in 1887 to confirm 140 people. A year later the parishioners petitioned the archbishop to establish a Diocesan Fund to assist the building of churches and the running of schools in sparsely populated areas, such as the Heidelberg Mission. While approving the proposal, Archbishop Carr noted that "Heidelberg does not belong in the category of poor parishes." He added that "they were sufficiently numerous and in circumstances sufficiently comfortable to adequately support their own school." His reflection possibly failed to appreciate the number of churches that had — and would be built — in the region of the Heidelberg Mission. As late as the 1920s, there were only about 180 families in the actual parish which included Templestowe and Ivanhoe.

Church construction included extensions to the mother church of the Heidelberg Mission, St John the Evangelist. William Wardell's design had not been completed in 1861. Almost half a century later, the building was too small for the number of parishioners, leading Fr Parker to propose the completion of the original plans. Following his arrival from Powlett River in South Gippsland in 1907, Fr Parker noted that "some £10,000-£12,000" was required to renovate the parish properties, including the presbytery as they "had got into a backward condition." Even though the parish was in debt of some £5,000, the archbishop approved the borrowing to complete the edifice. The renewed confidence and growing population motivated parishioners to once again raise funds for the construction.

The 1909 extensions

In 1909, the extensions were opened by the Vicar-General of the Archdiocese, Fr Patrick Phelan. They were in accord with the original design, adding two sections to the nave, a choir loft and organ, and a rear foyer and door. The additions almost doubled the seating capacity in the nave. A confessional was placed in the rear of the church. A new roof of Welsh slate and other renovations were also made at the time.

The present altar was also installed. Constructed from limestone, it features three beautifully carved front panels depicting the Sacrifice of Abraham, the Crucifixion and the Sacrifice of Melchizedek and an ornate reredos — the back wall of the high altar. This section of the 1909 altar was moved forward to its current location in the 1970s, replacing a wooden table which had been introduced following the liturgical changes flowing from the Second Vatican Council (1962-65). The stained-glass windows were also installed during and after the 1909 extensions.

A large gathering of people was in attendance for the opening of the completed church, with many people travelling from the far-flung reaches of the Heidelberg Mission to be present. Donations of £540 towards the £2,000 cost of the extension were made on the day.

Speaking of the architects at the opening, Fr Phelan, remarked: "So beautifully has the new work been dovetailed into the old, and so faithfully have they carried out the original idea [of William Wardell, who died in 1899], that whether one looks at the exterior or interior an entirely new church presents itself to the view."

Fr Phelan, who had expected to be made an auxiliary bishop in Melbourne, was to be appointed Bishop of Sale three years later. He thanked the parishioners of St John's, noting "the sacrifices which you faithful, generous people have made and are prepared to make . . ." He subsequently raised significant funds for the building of Newman College at the University of Melbourne, St Patrick's College, Sale and Corpus Christi seminary at Werribee.

The extension to the St John the Evangelist church is the reason why there are two blessing stones: the first on the south wall marking the celebration by Dr James Quinn, the Bishop of

Brisbane on the 4th May, 1860; and the second on the east wall by Dr Thomas Carr, the Archbishop of Melbourne on the 5th September 1909 marking the completion of the church.

In addition, there is a brass plaque in the entry foyer celebrating the consecration of the church by Dr George Pell, the Archbishop of Melbourne on 21st April 2001 during the 150th celebrations of St John the Evangelist. The then parish priest, Fr Anthony Girolami had discovered that although completed almost a century earlier, the church had never been consecrated!

Fr Parker was to remain at St John the Evangelist until 1915. In June that year, he was selected by Dr Carr to lead the fundraising effort for the construction of Newman College at the University of Melbourne, an engagement he undertook with considerable enthusiasm. Speaking at his farewell from Heidelberg, Dr Kenny observed that he:

> had won a warm place in their hearts ... including many of those who did not worship at the same altar ... his tireless energy and vigorous appeals ... throughout the district ... (his) name was spoken of in the highest terms of respect and the marvellous progress of Heidelberg parish under his guidance was the wonder and admiration of all.

Fr Parker — who lived on for another 17 years after retiring from Heidelberg — responded, saying the Heidelberg "was one of the most beautiful and most healthy suburbs of Melbourne and there was a great future in store for the district now that the land

... had been thrown open instead of being locked up by a few squatters." Near the end of his pastorate at Heidelberg, the strain on the parish lessened with the establishment of a separate parish at Diamond Greek with responsibility for Eltham, Warrandyte, Panton Hill, Arthur's Creek and Kinglake West.

Although the church of St John the Evangelist remains as it was completed in 1909, internal changes have been made from time to time, as detailed in later chapters. While retaining the historical character of the church, the changes have been mostly liturgical, following the reforms of Vatican II. By 1913, expenditure since Fr Parker's arrival had amounted to £13,000, of which £4,500 had been spent on schools. The parish debt had also been reduced to £3,800, an indication of the ongoing fundraising activities of the parishioners.

With the depression of the 1890s in the past and the Commonwealth of Australia a reality, the new nation celebrated an exciting new century. While the emerging conflict between capital and labour was leading to anarchy and revolutions elsewhere, Australians sought practical solutions to their new challenges. In the *Harvester* Case, Justice Higgins established a concept of a working wage for the family, a decision that reflected the social justice teachings of Pope Leo XIII in his 1891 encyclical, *Rerum Novarum* – the 'Rights and Duties of Capital and Labour.'

8

Arrival of the Sisters of Mercy and Daniel Mannix

Speaking at the opening of the completed extension to St John the Evangelist in 1909, the Vicar-General, Fr Patrick Phelan foreshadowed the next major challenge facing the parishioners of the parish and surrounding regions: "One duty remains to complete the trinity of great works. You have a comfortable home for the priests labouring in your midst. You have a church worthy of your faith, but the crown of your labours will be when you get a religious order to take the responsibility of educating your children ..."

Fr Phelan was referring to the impending arrival of the Sisters of Mercy at Heidelberg: "I am safe in saying that you may look forward to the arrival of the Sisters at the beginning of next year ... Your children and your children's children will be provided with teachers who will not only educate them for citizenship of this world, but prepare them also for that higher citizenship beyond the grave."

Established in Dublin by Catherine McAuley in 1831, the first Mercy Sisters journeyed to Perth in 1845. Three Sisters travelled to Melbourne in 1857 where they established the first Convent of Mercy in Victoria and the Academy of Mary Immaculate school in Nicholson Street, Fitzroy.

In January 1910, five Sisters, led by Sr Mary Basil, moved to 'Roma', a house in Cape Street, Heidelberg and commenced teaching at the primary school. They also began secondary school classes for six pupils in a room of their house.

The Order wasted little time in constructing a new wooden Parish Superior (Secondary) School which was opened in May 1911 with 14 pupils, both girls and boys. When later registered as Our Lady's College, it catered exclusively for girls. The Convent of Mercy was also built in 1911. The completed building was blessed by Archbishop Carr on the 24th September, the Feast of Our Lady of Mercy. The Sisters took up residence the following month. The Sisters soon expanded their presence when a new church and convent chapel were built at Eltham in 1912. They subsequently expanded their activities to teaching in other suburbs, visitations to the Austin Hospital and teaching music. The order established a Novitiate on Rosanna Road in the 1930s.

Mannix arrives in Melbourne

On Easter Sunday, 23rd March 1913, there occurred an event that was to mark the beginning of a momentous period in the life of the Church and nation. It was the arrival in Melbourne by train from Adelaide of Dr. Daniel Mannix, who had been appointed Coadjutor to Archbishop Carr. Mannix had sailed to Australia from Dublin before making the train journey to Melbourne where he would serve for the next 50 years, 46 of which he was Archbishop of Melbourne. A server at the first Mass celebrated in Melbourne was a Heidelberg parishioner, Dr AL Kenny, a generous philanthropist who contributed to many Catholic causes. Augustine Kenny — a leading Catholic layman of the era — had emigrated from Ireland with his parents in 1870. He was the first resident surgeon at the Eye and Ear Hospital and later at St Vincent's Hospital until retiring to private practice in 1908. Dr Kenny was involved in many church and secular initiatives for which he was awarded a papal knighthood (KSG) and made a companion of St Michael and St George (CMG). He was a generous benefactor of many causes, including Newman College and St Mary's Hall at the University of Melbourne, as well as the Heidelberg Mission.

The first recorded visit by the new bishop to St John the Evangelist occurred in May 1914, when Dr Mannix blessed the four glass-stained windows high above the sanctuary altar. The windows were dedicated to the memory of former pastors of the parish. Mannix was to visit Heidelberg many more times, including a few months after being installed as the Archbishop of Melbourne.

Mannix became the 3rd Archbishop of Melbourne in 1917. He had served as the president of St Patrick's College, Maynooth, Ireland's national seminary — where he had been educated — since 1903. With a large Irish Catholic population in Melbourne, Mannix was an obvious appointment, although it appears that he was never consulted about accepting the position.

The Great War

A year after the arrival of Dr Mannix in Melbourne, conflict broke out in Europe that would consume the world for the next four years and cost the lives of millions of people. Now known as the Great War, the conflict had a particular impact on the collective psyche of the Australian people. It was a war far from our shores; one that ended in retreat from Gallipoli; and in a simpering surrender on the Western Front after years of bloodshed in which some 25 million people died.

Consider the numbers: In 1914, the population of Australia was 4 million; Almost 417,000 people enlisted for the war – one in every ten people in the country; four in ten males between the age of 18 and 44 enlisted.

Of the 417,000: 58,000 were killed; 167,000 were wounded; 4,000 were missing or prisoners of war; and 88,000 suffered from sickness. In other words, there was a casualty rate of 65 per cent – the highest casualty rate of any nation engaged in WWI. To put this in today's context, it would involve almost a million Australians killed or wounded, as a proportion of our population. Inscribed on cenotaphs across Australia are the names of tens of thousands of young men who never returned from the conflict. Over 112,000 young Victorians enlisted. The memorial at Heidelberg lists the names of 30 young men who died in the Great War. The nearby cenotaph at Ivanhoe lists another 46 young men. The total population of Heidelberg and Ivanhoe at the time was about 4,000 persons. Across the river at Templestowe, there are 13 names of locals who never returned from the conflict. They lie in the gullies of Gallipoli, or in Flanders Fields, or some unknown places. These young men had carried the hopes and dreams of their families and local communities. The Anzac experience was seared into the Australian psyche.

As Geoffrey Blainey wrote in his *Short History of the World:* "From crowded apartments in Moscow to sheep farms in New Zealand there were millions of mantelpieces on which stood framed black-and-white photographs of earnest or smiling young men, killed in the war which everyone now called the Great War, not realising that a greater war was barely 20 years ahead."

Amongst those who volunteered from the small "dairying township" of Heidelberg was Fr Michael McKenna. A graduate of Xavier College, St Patrick's Seminary, Manly and Propaganda Fide College, Rome, Fr McKenna volunteered for active duty. An eye condition however precluded him from full duty. Instead, he was appointed a chaplain for the first voyage of Australian troops to the conflict, returning some months later to take up the role of parish priest at Heidelberg in 1915.

The proposed conscription of young men to serve in the war was a controversial issue, with Daniel Mannix a vocal opponent of Prime Minister Billy Hughes' push to introduce it. Hughes' decision to target the archbishop made Dr Mannix a household name, giving him a political prominence surpassing almost every other prelate in Australia. Later a strong opponent of communism, Mannix continued to attract attention and controversy throughout his long reign as the Archbishop of Melbourne.

9

Expanding Catholic Education

The outbreak of the Great War resulted in suspicion of local German families, many of them Lutherans who had settled in the region. A 24-hour guard was placed in the old Heidelberg bridge in fear of it being blown-up. Across the Yarra River in Doncaster and Templestowe, the street names were changed from Wilhelm and Bismark Streets, and German Lane to King, Victoria and George Streets. Regrettably some of the cooperation between Christian denominations — that had been prominent in the 1800s — waned and, in many instances, sectarianism was rife.

After the parish priest, Fr McKenna returned to Australia, he was appointed chaplain to the large military encampment at Heidelberg Heights, in addition to his parish and Heidelberg Mission duties. Captain McKenna, dressed in his military chaplain's uniform, was often seen riding to and from the camp. Described as "a worthy pastor" and one of "a fine body of Australian born pastors who were carrying on the work of the pioneer Irish priests with great success," Fr Mckenna built a church at Ivanhoe and purchased land for another at Templestowe. He had also reduced the parish debt from £4,500 and £2,100.

Marking the signing of the Armistice on 11th November 1918, celebrations were held across the nation, including a mighty bonfire on Eaglemont Hill.

It was some years after the Great War before life returned to normal. A few months after the end of the conflict, the 'Spanish flu' spread in Australia, leading to many deaths, including amongst local residents. It was a common sight at St John's for parishioners to attend liturgies wearing gauze masks soaked in eucalyptus or camphor. Towards the end of his tenure at Heidelberg, Fr McKenna introduced a monthly Mass at the Austin Hospital.

Away from the controversies surrounding the War, Archbishop Mannix laboured to expand the Catholic Church in Melbourne, especially the construction of schools and other educational institutions. Newman College, a residential college at the University of Melbourne, was opened in 1918, and Corpus Christi Seminary, Werribee in 1922.

Newman College was designed by Walter Burley Griffin and his wife Marion Mahoney, who had won the competition to design the nation's capital, Canberra. The Griffins lived in Heidelberg for a few years, designing a number houses that still exist on the Glenard Estate. A rare example of their inexpensive knitlock house was built at 52 Darebin Street. It was the home of noted war artist Murray Vaughan Griffin between 1922 and 1939.

The expansion of churches and schools

Locally, the building programs resumed after the end of the war. A presbytery was constructed at Diamond Creek, leading to the separation of that parish from the Mission. A new red brick church, dedicated to the Immaculate Conception, was opened at Ivanhoe, although Masses were still celebrated by the Heidelberg priest.

By 1920, there were 70 pupils at Our Lady's secondary school and a university class had been formed. Modern conveniences were slowly added. A telephone was installed at the convent in 1921, and electric lighting to the school and convent the following year. A tennis court was also opened at the school by a parishioner, Edmond Kiernan MLC.

The Sisters of Mercy opened a new school in Ivanhoe in 1922, comprising two class rooms, a cloak room and a lunch room for the sisters. By the end of the year, 53 pupils were attending the school.

In 1924, Mr P Finn presented the Order with a block of land in Yarra Street, Heidelberg, which enabled the expansion of the school facilities. He also generously provided the land for the Sisters of Mercy Novitiate in Rosanna.

Fr McKenna was transferred to Elwood in early 1922, to be replaced by Fr Thomas Joseph Power. He would be the parish priest until 1929. Born in Kilkenny and educated at All Hallows College, Dublin, Fr Power arrived in Australia in 1909. He served in a number of parishes as Assistant Priest before his appointment to Heidelberg.

Renewed optimism returned to the community in the 1920s as many people sought to escape the stringencies of the previous decade. Fundraising activities, which had been a constant burden for the parishioners for decades, were renewed to meet new demands, especially a new primary school. The existing St Monica's Primary School, which had been built in 1871 to replace the original one-room structure, was overcrowded and inadequate. Fundraising bazaars were a regular feature of parish life. When Fr Power arrived at Heidelberg, the parish carried a £2,000 debt, "but the new school at Ivanhoe and other works added £4,500 to the liability." Archbishop Mannix was to observe that "it is a remarkable thing about this and other parishes that the old debts are not cleared off before fresh debts are contracted."

On 17th June 1928, Archbishop Mannix laid the foundation stone for a new school, placed under the patronage of St John the Evangelist. The building progressed quickly, with the new five classroom school being completed that year. The new school could accommodate 300 pupils. The construction also included St John's Hall with a capacity for 400 people. The red brick hall has been used since then for parish, school and other activities.

In 1924, the locals cheered when a parishioner, Bill Twomey, won the prestigious Stawell Gift. Three of his sons, Pat, Mick and Bill, played football for Collingwood. Many other parishioners have excelled in sport and other endeavours over the decades. John Lanigan became a leading tenor at London's Covent Garden Opera House. Winifred O'Sullivan became an acclaimed international pianist. Thousands of others contributed to the parish, the community and government, and other endeavours through the years. Many became priests or joined religious orders, including Sr Miriam Vaughan OCDM, a daughter of a previous historian of the parish, Eileen Vaughan.

As the decade of the 1920s drew to a close, dark clouds gathered over the world economy. The Great Depression was to engulf the globe, as production fell, unemployment soared and masses of people were reduced to poverty. A political crisis eventuated with the Labor Government of James Scullin falling, to be replaced by the new United Australia Party led by former Labor Acting Treasurer, Joseph Lyons. Lyons, in partnership with former members of the conservative Nationalist Party piloted Australia through some of its most difficult years, emerging from the depression earlier than many other countries including the United States of America.

The pre-Vatican II sanctuary (St John's archives)

10

Depression and War

Despite the Great Depression, the work of evangelisation continued in the parish, especially in the field of education.

The Sisters of Mercy connection to Heidelberg was cemented with the opening of their new Noviciate in 1930. Standing on a ridge at Rosanna, the impressive three-story building became the home of new members of the order for decades. Some 10,000 people flocked to the grounds for the opening by the Apostolic Delegate. Many of the young noviciates assisted with teaching at the local Mercy schools as part of their training and formation. The following year, the sisters celebrated the centenary of the founding of the Order in Dublin in 1831.

Parishioners engaged in various social outreach projects during the era, many of them necessitated by the Great Depression. A conference of the Society of St Vincent de Paul had been formed at St John the Evangelist in 1927, and has assisted the poor and needy ever since.

The Catholic Women's Social Guild — the members of which were dedicated to assisting the elderly — was formed locally in 1930. A branch of the Catholic Young Men's Society was active in the 1930s, organising many sporting and social events.

A weekly envelope giving system was introduced in the 1930s to assist with the raising of the funds necessary to finance the parish. Additional funds were required when a fire caused extensive damage to the sacristy, the nun's chapel and the roofing of the sanctuary in 1931. Mass was celebrated in the hall while repairs were undertaken over the following month.

With the population of the area continuing to expand, Heidelberg was proclaimed a city in November 1934. A year later, local residents joined with others to celebrate the centenary of Melbourne. The major Catholic contribution was a National Eucharistic Congress which attracted tens of thousands of participants to Victoria's capital city. The same year, the Society of Jesus established a seminary at Watsonia, which operated until 1974.

In the 1930s a group of painters gathered at *Heide*, a dairy farm belonging to John and Sunday Reed, across the Yarra River from Heidelberg, to form a new artists colony. Now familiar names, the artists — including Sidney Nolan, Albert Tucker, Joy Hester and Arthur Boyd — reinterpreted the Australian landscape and their experiences of living in Australia half a century after the original

The Heidelberg Mission and St John the Evangelist

Heidelberg school.

Fr James Norris had been appointed parish priest in 1929, a position he was to occupy for 16 years. Born in Carlton, he was educated in Melbourne before attending St Patrick's Seminary at Manly, NSW. He had served in a number of parishes before his appointment to Heidelberg. During the 1933 celebrations of the 80th anniversary of the parish, it was said of him that "he never spared himself."

Amongst his activities was the celebration of a monthly Mass at the Austin Hospital. The hospital had opened in 1882 as a hospital for incurables with a very generous gift of £6,000 from Mrs. Thomas Austin. It expanded over the years, offering more and more services, training for nurses and general training for doctors. From the very earliest days, the priests at St John the Evangelist provided chaplaincy services to the hospital. They also served the Mont Park Psychiatric Hospital. From 1940, the chaplain to the Rosanna Convent was also formally attached to the parish.

Fr Norris also installed the current Stations of the Cross — made in the Opus Sectile style of inlay – in memory of Thomas Jordan whose widow donated the funds. The original stations were moved to St Joseph's church, Wonthaggi, along with a number of gas lights. The crosses above the new set are from the original stations.

On Good Friday 1939, Australia's 10th Prime Minister, Joseph Lyons died in office. He had dragged the nation out of the Great Depression. By the time Australia had emerged from the downturn, another global catastrophe was looming — the Second World War — a conflict which would come to the nation's doorstep.

World War II

It was on the 3rd September 1939 that Prime Minister Robert Menzies informed his "Fellow Australians" that "it is my melancholy duty to inform you officially that, in consequence of the persistence of Germany in her invasion of Poland, Great Britain has declared war upon her, and that, as a result, Australia is also at war. No harder task can fall to the lot of a democratic leader than to make such an announcement."

Menzies had replaced Lyons as the prime minister, but was to lose government to Labor leader, John Curtin in 1941. Curtin was also to die in office four years later. He was replaced by Ben Chifley, a former train driver, the nation's third Catholic prime minister.

The conflict reached Australia's shores with the bombing of Darwin, Japanese submarines in Sydney Harbour and a great naval battle in the Coral Sea. It wrought havoc on communities across the country, just as the Great War had done two decades earlier. Almost 40,000 Australians were killed in the conflict, including many from the Heidelberg area.

Before war broke out, accommodation at St John's Primary School was becoming overcrowded. Wartime shortages of both materials and labour precluded expansion. The sisters had to cope with congestion with the classrooms built in 1928 overflowing. St Monica's was used again as a school room. In the hall, a class was conducted on the stage and three on the floor. It wasn't until years after the war concluded that new classrooms were constructed as the country continued to suffer major shortages and rationing. In 1940, Ivanhoe was separated from Heidelberg as a parish.

A year before the war concluded in 1945, a new priest was appointed to Heidelberg. He was Fr Patrick Power, who had attended the same schools in Ireland as his predecessor before emigrating to Australia. He too served in a number of parishes before his appointment to Heidelberg, the most recent at Castlemaine.

A feature of the church of St John the Evangelist is the large stained-glass windows above the reredos at the west end of the church. The main panels are dedicated to four Parish Priests, Frs Hoyle (1858-62), Finn (1862-77), O'Callaghan (1882- 1907) and Parker (1907-15). The first three depict the Annunciation, the Baptism of Christ and the Crucifixion. The last one, depicting the Ascension, was blessed by Archbishop Daniel Mannix in 1947.

Apart from the panel of stained-glass windows above the altar and the rose window of St John the Evangelist above the choir loft, the other windows were donated by local individuals and families. The window in the sanctuary depicts the three wise men with Joseph, Mary and the child Jesus. Those in the nave depict the Sacred Heart, the Agony in the Garden, Mary Magdalen washing the feet of Jesus, Jesus calming the storm, Jesus blessing little children, and the Holy Family. They were installed in the 1940s.

The end of the war increased the workload for the Heidelberg priests. Parishioners also contributed to the hospital mission, including wheeling patients to the monthly masses. In addition to the chaplaincy at the Austin Hospital, a new repatriation hospital was opened on Waterdale Road in 1941 to cope with injured service men and women. By 1947, the Commonwealth hospital had 2,000 beds and a staff of 1,200. The new office of the chaplain to the repatriation hospital was formally attached to the parish that year. It was subsequently transferred to the parish of St Pius X in 1953. The parish also served an emergency housing estate which had been established on the deserted Watsonia military camp, as well as other temporary housing at Mont Park.

The Melbourne archdiocese celebrated its centenary in May 1948. Tens of thousands of the faithful attended the weeklong events at which special guests included Cardinal Spellman from New York, Irish President Eamon de Valera and the famous Scottish tenor, Fr Sydney McEwan. With the war over, a new optimism spread across the nation.

11

Post-war expansion

Long before the Second World War had ended, Australia's leaders recognised that they had to increase the population of the nation significantly if they were to secure its future. 'Populate or perish' was the catch cry that gained increasing prominence from the 1930s.

This realisation resulted in two major programs: a large influx of immigrants in the post-war period; and the replacement of the inadequate housing in the inner suburbs of the capital cities.

The post-war immigration program began in earnest in 1945. Assisted passages helped many families make the long trip from Europe.

The demand for housing for the new migrants resulted in the rapid expansion of Melbourne's suburbs. Vast tracts of land that had been farms were purchased for new estates as ship loads of 'new Australians' arrived.

For more than fifty years, the region around the villages of Doncaster and Templestowe had been used for market gardens and orchards. The area, where significant quantities of fresh fruit and vegetable were grown, was known as the 'food basket' of the city.

With the demand for housing growing rapidly, these farms were being purchased for new estates. Over the following decades, the farms were replaced by suburban housing. Rapid urbanisation following the war transformed Heidelberg from a rural village to a suburban centre.

Some 4.2 million migrants arrived between 1945 and 1985, 40 per cent of which were from the UK and Ireland. There were many from other parts of the continent: Italy, Greece, the Netherlands, and from people fleeing persecution in Eastern Europe. Many of these immigrants settled in nearby Doncaster and Templestowe.

The rapid expansion of these suburbs resulted in demand for services. Many of the new citizens were Christians including Roman Catholics from Italy and Orthodox Christians from Greece and Eastern Europe. Before long, they were seeking places to worship and educate their children.

These developments placed new pressures on the Heidelberg Mission.

A church for Templestowe

For some years, Mass had been celebrated in the Memorial Hall at Templestowe to save parishioners the journey to Heidelberg, especially when petrol was rationed during the War. In earlier years, they had travelled the 11 kilometres by horse and on foot!

After the conflict, a wooden hut that had been used by the US military was purchased and moved to the suburb. It was a difficult move for Louis Arthur, a parishioner and well-known Melbourne transport operator, manoeuvring the building across the Yarra River and uphill to its new location.

The hut was renovated and blessed by Archbishop Mannix in June 1947. It was dedicated to St Kevin as a memorial to the 21-year Kevin Sheahan — from a third generation Templestowe family — who was killed on Moratai Island while serving in the RAAF. Mannix was effusive about the location. Surveying the surrounding rolling hills and gullies of Templestowe, he observed: "I am delighted to stand here and survey the countryside; the view could be scarcely surpassed in any part of Australia."

The original wooden structure was later moved to Park Orchards where it was dedicated to St Anne. Templestowe was detached from the Heidelberg Mission in 1960 as part of a new East Doncaster Parish, which would ultimately include Bulleen, Doncaster and Donvale.

Two years after the opening of St Kevin's Templestowe, a new church dedicated to St Bernadette was opened at Ivanhoe West as housing in the suburb expanded towards Darebin Creek. That expansion resulted in the construction of the new parish of St Pius X at Heidelberg West in 1953. Until a presbytery was built 12 years later, the first priest, Fr George Maher resided with a Heidelberg parishioner. Fr Maher had originally been appointed to Coburg, but was swapped at the last moment by the Vicar-General, Fr Arthur Fox with Fr Vin Arthur on the basis that the latter had been a parishioner at Heidelberg.

In 1957, the housing boom led to the opening of the Mother of God church in East Ivanhoe. Fr Patrick O'Connor, who had been appointed to Heidelberg in 1949, oversaw these developments. He had been educated by the Sisters of Mercy and the Christian Brothers at Tralee and the National University, Dublin before travelling to Australia.

The building activity was not confined to new churches. The Christian Brothers Parade College Preparatory School was opened at Alphington in 1952. A new brick wing for Our Lady of Mercy College was completed in 1954. Much needed additional classrooms were finally built for St John's Primary School. The four new rooms were used by pupils from many lands, including Poland, Italy, the UK, Hungary, Lithuania, Latvia, Germany, Russia, Holland and the Ukraine. The class composition reflected the post-war immigration to Australia. Student numbers grew in the 1950s. In 1955, there were 504 pupils enrolled at St John's primary school.

The purchase of adjoining properties had allowed the expansion of the school. The tennis courts were relocated to their present place as a part of the development.

A new primary school was built at Macleod in 1956. Dedicated to St Martin of Tours, it served as a temporary church until a permanent structure was built in 1973.

The 1950s was a decade of considerable change. The Elizabethan era commenced when the 25-year-old Princess became Queen and ascended the throne in 1953. The world spotlight shone on Melbourne for the Olympic Games in 1956, with the athletes housed at West Heidelberg. The world was projected into Australian living rooms with the arrival of television in the country. The Menzies government presided over an era of economic expansion. The nation thrived. It was the beginning of a new generation — the 'baby boomers' — that would influence the country for half a century.

The altar relief depicting the Sacrifice of Abraham, the Crucifixion and the Sacrifice of Melchizedek (The author) and the statue of St Mary of the Cross MacKillop (The author)

12

Social upheaval and liturgical change

As the fifties drew to a close, a momentous event in the 2,000-year-old history of the Catholic Church was announced. It was the Second Vatican Council, a process still having reverberations more than 60 years later. Announced by the newly elected Pope John XXIII, the Council was to run from October 1962 until December 1965.

The Council produced 16 major documents which reiterated and updated the role of the church for the modern era. In many ways, it continued the work that commenced with the first Vatican Council (1869-70) which had ended prematurely with the *Risorgimento* — the reunification of Italy and the abolition of the Papal States in 1871. One of the items never reached by the first council was the role of the laity.

By the time the Council concluded, John XXIII had died. He was succeeded as pope by Paul VI who visited Australia in 1970. It was the first papal visit to the country.

Two major changes made at the Vatican Council affected the Catholics in Heidelberg — and around the world. First, the new Mass — *Novus Ordo Missae* — could be said in the vernacular language, leading to widespread change from Latin to English. Secondly, the priest could face the congregation, resulting in the placement of a low altar in the sanctuary. Communicants no longer had to fast overnight, and Extraordinary Ministers of the Eucharist were permitted with large congregations.

At St John's, the altar rails were removed by the then parish priest, Fr Coghlan, opening the sanctuary to the nave. A wooden altar had been installed, allowing the priest to celebrate the Mass facing the congregation. Unlike many churches, the existing high altar was retained and its table was moved forward to its current position in the 1970s.

Looking back, it can be difficult to appreciate the magnitude of the changes. The parishioners at Heidelberg had only known the traditional Latin Mass. In one short period, generations of understanding and experience had been swept aside. Many welcomed the changes as they enabled greater participation in the liturgy, but others were regretful that something they considered sacred had been usurped. It was a time of mixed emotions that required sensitive care from the pastors at St John the Evangelist.

Two priests served the parish during the decade: Fr Bernard Payne from 1960, and Fr Mortimer Fitzgerald from 1965. Fr Payne had been born at Abbotsford and was educated at Parade and St Kevin's colleges before attending Corpus Christi seminary, Werribee. He was very supportive of parish social and spiritual groups, reforming the Catholic Women's Social Guild amongst other endeavours. He also published a parish gazette, *Lumen Christi*. Like his predecessors, he was devoted to fundraising to repay debts on the school and renovations to the church.

His successor, Fr Mortimer Fitzgerald had been born at Korumburra before attending St Patrick's College, Sale. He completed his studies at Corpus Christi Seminary. Fr Fitzgerald oversaw the modernisation of the presbytery, the installation of a pipe organ and the construction of the current tennis courts after the demolition of an old house that had occupied the site. The layout of the presbytery gardens was also undertaken by Fr Mortimer.

The last church

The decision to create a new parish in Bulleen in 1962 marked the end of an era, for it was the last in the area to be carved directly from the original Heidelberg Mission. A new school was also planned, but until it could be constructed, St Monica's was pressed into use again for three junior classes for children bussed to and from Bulleen each day.

Fr John Spillane was appointed Priest of the Bulleen parish, but it wasn't until a decade later that the new church dedicated to St Clement of Rome was opened in 1972. The new suburb was the home of numerous Italian migrants — an enterprising group — of which many were engaged in the building and construction industry, who purchased 16 acres of land on the Yarra River in 1969, opening the specially designed Veneto Club in 1973.

A new church was constructed at Ivanhoe in 1962 to replace the previous brick building. A feature of the modern structure was the commissioning of a triptych of *The Annunciation, the Virgin Enthroned and the Visitation* by the Blake Prize winning artist, Justin O'Brien. However, the Parish Priest didn't like it, selling the painting to Fr Michael Scott SJ, the Rector of Newman College, where it now adorns the High Table in the grand dining room!

The end of an era

Just a few months before his 100th birthday in 1963, Daniel Mannix died, having been the Archbishop of Melbourne for 46 years. His remarkable time in Melbourne had already been preceded by a significant contribution to the church in Ireland, serving as the President of St Patrick's College, at the National University, Maynooth. His long tenure in Melbourne was marked by the significant expansion of the Church, and the creation of the modern Catholic education system.

Mannix was replaced by his coadjutor, Justin Simmons, the fifth Archbishop of Hobart (1937-42). Simmons, who had served as the coadjutor bishop of Melbourne from 1942 until 1963, was the first Australian-born head of the church in Melbourne, marking the ending of the century-long Irish influence on the local episcopate. Having waited 22 years to become Archbishop, Simmons was in the role for just four years.

In July 1968, Catholics globally became aware of what was to become perhaps the most discussed papal encyclical of all time, *Humanae Vitae*. The document, 'On Human Life', had been anticipated by some as an accommodation by the Church of modern mores, especially about marriage and sexuality. Some were disappointed that the pope reiterated the Church's traditional teachings, a position reinforced by each of his successors.

Following the death of Archbishop Simmons in 1967, James Knox was appointed his successor. Born in Western Australia, he was educated at the Benedictine Abbey at New Norcia and the Pontifical Urban University. A long time Vatican diplomat, who had served in Kenya and India, Knox was to be appointed Australia's first Cardinal in 1973. He returned to Rome the following year to head the Congregation for Divine Worship and Discipline of the Sacraments before being appointed the president of the Pontifical Council for the Family in 1981. Cardinal Knox died in 1983.

Cardinal Knox's legacy in Melbourne included the reorganisation of the Archdiocese, including the appointment of regional bishops and the creation of the Melbourne College of Divinity.

He also oversaw the 40th International Eucharistic Conference in 1973 to which many parishioners from Heidelberg joined others from throughout the nation and overseas for the events.

A decade of change

The cultural revolution of the 1960s impacted society and church. It was the decade that the Beatles visited Melbourne; and the model Jean Shrimpton scandalised the establishment by wearing an above-the-knee dress to the Melbourne Cup.

Australia's longest serving prime minister, Sir Robert Menzies retired — and his successor, Harold Holt went missing off Portsea. The nation overwhelmingly voted to remove discrimination against the indigenous people in the Constitution in 1967 and an aborigine, Lionel Rose won a world boxing belt. Women no longer had to leave the public service upon marriage. The Vietnam War was underway with young men conscripted to National Service. Lyndon Johnson became the first US President to visit Australia.

The pupils at St John's Primary School learnt how to count with the new decimal currency in 1966. Three years later they gathered to watch grainy black and white images of Neil Armstrong take a "giant step for mankind" when he walked on the moon.

13

The End of the Irish Era

With the opening of St Clement of Rome church at Bulleen, the focus of the Heidelberg parishioners returned to the needs of St John the Evangelist. Once again, the primary school was overcrowded and in need of more classrooms. This task fell to Fr Michael Sheehy, who was appointed the parish priest in 1972.

Born at Duagh in County Kerry, Fr Sheehy was educated at the Jesuit seminary, Limerick and St Patrick's College, Carlow before his ordination and journey to Melbourne where he served in a series of parishes before his appointment to Heidelberg. Fr Sheehy had the distinction of being the last Irish born and educated priest to serve at St John the Evangelist, marking the ending of a century-long tradition.

In addition to his pastoral interests, Michael Sheehy was an accomplished sportsman, playing Gaelic football for Kerry in the All Ireland League in his youth. More importantly — for his role at Heidelberg — he had a keen interest in economics and administration. These skills were to come to the fore in the expansion of the school.

Although the expansion of the school was urgent, neither the Archdiocesan Schools Provident Fund nor banks would advance the funds necessary for the project. Undeterred, Fr Sheehy pressed ahead. He designed a scheme, known as the Parish Purse whereby parishioners could loan funds at better than the interest rates charged by the banks. A considerable amount was raised. He also purchased a house and land in Yarra Street as a 'safety valve' should it be required.

As a consequence of this initiative, four additional classrooms were constructed. In recent decades, St John the Evangelist was fortunate to have the services of parishioner architects, Max Chester and Frank Viola to design meeting rooms and new classrooms. Renovations were also undertaken to the church, including the installation of better lighting and an organ console at the front of the nave. Renovations were also undertaken at the old St Monica's. In seven and a half years, the parish debt was cleared.

There were 609 families in the parish at the beginning of the 1970s. In addition to the capital works on the school and church, Fr Sheehy was active in the promotion of various groups, including a teenage group, and a hospitality group.

With the appointment of Cardinal Knox to Rome in 1974, the See of Melbourne became vacant. It was filled by Thomas Francis Little, the sixth Archbishop of Melbourne, a position he held until his retirement 22-years later in 1996. Knighted in 1977, Archbishop Sir Frank Little established the deanery system and oversaw the development of the parishes and laity through programs such as Renew.

Social change

The changes in cultural and social mores of the 60s were reflected in events of the following decade. The *Family Law Act* allowed no-fault divorce; civil marriage celebrants were introduced; Australia's first IVF baby was born in 1980; Germaine Greer authored *The Female Eunuch*; and compulsory maternity leave was introduced. Young people were given the vote at 18 years of age; and a little-known actor, Mel Gibson, who was the make a film about the *The Passion of the Christ*, starred in the first *Mad Max* film. A grand Opera House was opened in Sydney. Politically, the election of the Whitlam government ended 27 years of Liberal-National party rule and ushered in major policy changes, including free tertiary education and the Medibank health insurance scheme. It was a decade of significant change that impacted upon all Australians.

Following the controversial dismissal of the Whitlam Government in 1975, Malcolm Fraser's administration sought to address the economic challenges facing Australia. Significantly for the church, it opened the doors to Asian immigration, with some 200,000 people coming to Australia, including 56,000 from Vietnam, many of which were Catholics. The government established the Institute of Multicultural Affairs and the Special Broadcasting Service (SBS).

14

The Impact of John Paul II

In 1979, Fr Michael Sheehy was transferred from Heidelberg to Doncaster where he was engaged in the building of a new church dedicated to St Gregory the Great, the 64th Bishop of Rome. It was opened by Archbishop Little in December 1983. Fr Sheehy was replaced at Heidelberg by Fr Robert Coghlan who was born at Geelong, attending St Patrick's College and the Christian Brothers, before seminary studies at Werribee and the new Corpus Christi campus at Glen Waverley.

Fr Coghlan — then the youngest pastor appointed as parish priest at Heidelberg — replaced the post-Vatican II 'low' wooden altar with the table section of the original altar and removed the old confessional from the rear of the church. A talented musician, he sponsored a series of Charismatic Renewal events at St John the

Evangelist. He also restored the original church bell, mounting it over the chimney of the chapel.

A significant change also occurred at St John's Primary School in 1983 when the first lay principal was appointed. Seven decades after they came to St John the Evangelist in 1910, the long and faithful service of the Sisters of Mercy came to an end. The last religious principal was Sr Kathleen Mangan RSM, the daughter of parishioners who donated one of the stained-glass windows in the nave. She and Srs Antoinette Burke RSM and Patricia Fulton RSM were the last to teach at the school. There have been five lay principals to date: Mary Penny, Patricia Jones, Nick Marinelli, Maureen Stella and Alison Dean.

The change reflected in part the declining number of members of religious orders. Over seven decades, dozens of sisters had taught at the local schools. A number remained parishioners, including Sr Jean Walton RSM and Sr Loreto Lynch RSM, one of the church organists. A memorial labyrinth for contemplation and prayer was gifted to the church to celebrate the centenary of Our Lady of Mercy College in 2010 as an acknowledgement of the relationship between the school and the parish.

It was during this era that a new ecumenical welfare group, Heidelcare, was formed to provide voluntary assistance in the area. The group operated for more than three decades, serving the aged, disabled and others in need of assistance, such as transport to and from medical and other appointments.

Throughout this period, local parishes, such as St John the Evangelist, were touched by a global reawakening that had its origins in the Second Vatican Council and was rekindled by an extraordinary pope.

Pope John Paul II

The premature death of Pope John Paul I — just 33 days after his election in 1978 — resulted in the surprise election of Karol Wojtyla, the Cardinal Archbishop of Krakow, Poland. His election was only after the eighth ballot on the third day of the conclave. He was the first non-Italian pope for 455 years and would become the third longest serving pope after St Peter and Pius IX. He was also the youngest pope for more than a century.

Partly because of his clear message of evangelisation — and partly because of his longevity — John Paul II had a profound impact on both the church and the world. The latter is clear: his visit to his native Poland in June 1979 set in motion nine days that changed the course of history and led directly to the collapse of the Soviet Union and Eastern European communism. His witness to "live in the truth," as Václav Havel expressed it, resonated in the consciousness of his fellow Poles and millions of others globally.

John Paul II's impact on the church was also profound. While some people interpreted Vatican II as the church accommodating the cultural *zeitgeist*, John Paul II — and his successors — insisted that the purpose of the Council was to refocus Christians on their relationship with Jesus and the evangelising task of sanctifying the world.

This was the evangelising message of the most travelled pope in history, visiting 129 countries — many of them multiple times — including Australia twice. It was his message to the World Meetings of Families. It was his message to the millions of young people who attended World Youth Days. It was his message in the 129 Wednesday audiences that became the work now known as the *Theology of the Body*. As he wrote in the encyclical, *Redemptoris Missio*, "The moment has come to commit all of the Church's energies to the New evangelisation . . . No believer in Christ, no institution of the Church can avoid this supreme duty: to proclaim Christ to all peoples."

There were few Catholics globally untouched by John Paul II, including in Australia. Many young parishioners from St John the Evangelist parish have attended World Youth Days, and at least one of the families attended the World Meeting of Families with the Holy Father. St John's parishioners attended the Mass at Flemington Racecourse and the Ecumenical Service at the MCG during Pope John Paul II's visit in 1986. His 14 encyclicals attracted wide readership and his *Theology of the Body* deep study. Catholic institutes and colleges, such as the John Paul II Institute for Marriage and Family and Campion College have disseminated his writings.

The 1980s and 90s was an era of considerable change in Australia as the five pillars of the original national economic and cultural settlement — the White Australia policy, industry protection, wage arbitration, state paternalism and imperial benevolence — were abandoned or replaced by the Hawke-Keating and Howard-Costello governments. Many of the changes were — or remain — contested as the nation wrestles with a new settlement about its foundational civic and other values.

The church of St John the Evangelist — completed in 1909 with the Presbytery in the background (The author).

15

Renovations and Celebrations

With the approach of the 150th anniversary of the parish in 2001, thoughts turned to the state of the church building which was in need of major renovations. This task fell to Fr Barry Whelan, who was appointed to the parish in 1987. He had succeeded Fr James Atkins, who had been appointed to Heidelberg in 1984. Just three years after his move to Heidelberg, Fr Atkins died.

It was during this period that the most extensive renovations to the church were undertaken since its completion more than a century earlier. The building was closed for months while the interior was refurbished, with liturgical services conducted in the hall. The pews were removed and re-stained, new carpet laid, heating installed, the walls repainted, new cabinetry built in the sacristy, pipes and drainage repaired and the slate roof cleaned.

Celebrating the 150th anniversary

In 1995, Fr Anthony Girolami was appointed Parish Priest of Heidelberg, having previously served as the assistant priest. Raised in Coburg East and schooled at Trinity College, Brunswick and St Joseph's College, North Melbourne, Fr Girolami attended Corpus Christi College, Clayton.

Fr Girolami oversaw the celebrations for the 150th anniversary of the parish in 2001. A series of events were planned, including a commemorative Mass celebrated by Archbishop Pell, and a Ball at the Ivanhoe Centre.

In researching the history of the church, Fr Girolami discovered, that although the foundation stones had been blessed, the church had never been consecrated. This was rectified when the Archbishop of Melbourne, George Pell, consecrated the building in April 2001 as part of the joyous celebrations for the 150th anniversary. A very large congregation attended the Mass and a time capsule was placed under the floor of the rear foyer of the church.

Cardinal George Pell

Following the retirement of Frank Little as Archbishop of Melbourne in 1996, George Pell was appointed his successor. Born in Ballarat, he was educated at Loreto Convent and St Patrick's College before seminary studies at Corpus Christi, Werribee, the

Pontifical Urban University, Rome and Oxford. A talented sportsman, Pell played Australian Rules Football — signing with the Richmond Football Club — but ultimately pursued his religious vocation.

A kindly and thoughtful person, Pell had been an auxiliary bishop for nine years before his appointment to the Melbourne See, a position he held for five years before succeeding Cardinal Clancy in Sydney. During his time in Melbourne, he established new religious education guidelines and materials, to be used in schools such as St John's Primary. He also established the 'Protocols to investigate and address complaints of child sexual abuse', the first such response anywhere in the world. While in Sydney, he hosted the 12th World Youth Day to which some 500,000 people attended, including a group from St John the Evangelist, Heidelberg.

George Pell was made a Cardinal in 2003 by John Paul II and subsequently the Prefect for the Secretariat for the Economy by Pope Francis. In assuming the role, he became the highest ranking Australian in the Roman Curia ever, effectively the number three person in the Vatican. His discovery of millions of dollars in hidden accounts earned displeasure from some, but the applaud of many. He was unjustly convicted of alleged child sexual offences, a conviction that was unanimously quashed by Australia's High Court. Cardinal Pell died of complications of hip surgery in Rome in 2023.

Denis Hart succeeded George Pell as Archbishop of Melbourne

in 2001 a position he served in until retirement in 2018. Educated at St John's Hawthorn, Xavier College, Kew and Corpus Christi College, he had served as Auxiliary Bishop of Melbourne since 1997.

Fr Girolami made a number of changes to the interior of the church, including the installation of a large crucifix at the front of the nave. A crucifix had hung on the wall for many years until moved to the church grounds as a wayside shrine by Fr Fitzgerald in the late 1960s. It was subsequently provided with a cover and surrounding garden bed by Fr Coghlan in the 1980s.

The Fuller Organ

Thanks to the generosity of parishioners, Fr Girolami obtained a 'new' pipe organ for the church in 2000. Known as the Fuller organ — after its Kew manufacturer Alfred Fuller — the 510-pipe instrument had been a feature of St Mary's church, Echuca from 1890 until 1970 when it was moved to the chapel of St Mary's Redemptorist Monastery, at Wendouree, Ballarat. With the closure of the monastery, it was purchased for Heidelberg, restored to its original splendour and placed in the choir loft in 2000.

In 2011, Fr Anthony was appointed to the staff of Corpus Christi College, the Victorian seminary, which had been moved to Carlton from Clayton in 2000. His successor at Heidelberg was Fr Ted Teal.

The turn of the century

The decades bookending the turn of the century marked considerable changes in Australia. There were three decades of stable government, under Malcolm Fraser, Bob Hawke and Paul Keating and John Howard. A massacre at Port Arthur led to significant gun law reform; the High Court extended provisions relating to indigenous Australians in the *Mabo* and *Wik* cases; a referendum to establish an Australian Head of State was defeated; and the Northern Territory's euthanasia legislation was overturned by a Private Members Bill moved in the Commonwealth Parliament by a parishioner of St John the Evangelist.

Australians worried about a computer bug that never eventuated; many were killed or injured in the Bali and Jakarta bombings in Indonesia; and a citizenship test for immigrants was introduced. Global attention turned to Australia for the Sydney Olympics; and World Youth Day in 2000 was attended by Pope Benedict XVI and hundreds of thousands of young people, including young German pilgrims who were hosted by St John's before travelling to Sydney. In Rome, St Mary of the Cross MacKillop was canonised.

William Wardell born 1824-1899
(Taken from William Wardell: Building with Conviction, A. G. Evans).

16

The 21ˢᵗ Century

Following the excitement of the 150th celebrations, the parishioners of St John the Evangelist enjoyed the ambience of their renovated church. It was a period of consolidation and emphasis on the pastoral needs of parishioners.

Leading this effort was Fr Ted Teal, a gentle and quietly spoken man known for his pastoral care, who was appointed to Heidelberg in 2002, serving as Parish Priest until 2013.

Born at Lahore, India — now Pakistan — in 1941, Ted Teal, was the great, great grandson of Henry Teal, a British soldier who was stationed there in 1821. The Teals remained on the subcontinent, working in various occupations. Together with his parents, a young Ted emigrated to Australia in 1949 following the Indian partition two years earlier. He was schooled at Sacred Heart Primary School, Oakleigh and De La Salle, Malvern before studying at Corpus Christi Werribee and Glen Waverley.

Fr Ted composed the parish prayer which has been used since then. He also oversaw the reconstruction of the bluestone wall surrounding the church grounds, as well as restoring and relocating the original gates to the churchyard on the pathway to the presbytery.

Chaplaincy

The chaplaincy work for the priests at Heidelberg increased with the rebuilding of the local hospital complex. After 30 years in East Melbourne, the Mercy Hospital for Women moved to Heidelberg to form part of the new health complex with the adjoining, rebuilt Austin Hospital in 2005. In 2012, the Olivia Newton-John Cancer and Wellness Centre (ONJ) was opened as part of the hospital complex. The Grammy-winning singer and *Grease* star who developed breast cancer, donated much of her wealth to cancer projects, including the ONJ centre in Heidelberg.

Although the chaplaincy work was shared with the priest at St Pius X for many years, it was the reason why there was generally an assistant priest at Heidelberg. Dozens of priests have served as an Assistant at St John the Evangelist over the decades, including in recent years, Frs. John Pereira, John O'Connor, Albert Jogarajah, David Cartwright, Bill Edebols, Michael Moody and Patrick Purcell. Their work has been supported by a pastoral associate, Carlene McDevitt and Elizabeth Williamson; and a parish secretary, Marilyn McCann and Mary Peeris in recent years.

Following Fr Ted's retirement, Fr Mario Zammit became the parish priest. A member of the Missionary Society of St Paul — an order founded in Malta and which came to Australia in 1948 — Fr Mario had served as the Provincial of the Order in Australia before being posted to Heidelberg.

Fr Mario oversaw a refurbishment of parts of the presbytery, including the addition of the Francis Xavier room, a meeting space for parish activities.

He departed the Parish in 2021 to pursue missionary activities with his congregation in the Philippines.

The Covid Years

Fr Joel Peart came to St John the Evangelist in 2020. Educated at St Bernard's College, Essendon and Corpus Christi College, he had the misfortune that his appointment coincided with the outbreak of the Covid 19 virus in Australia. With the long and severe restrictions on gatherings and movements, church attendance became almost impossible for parishioners for more than a year. The social isolation had a negative impact on many people.

It was during this period that the archdiocese, under the leadership of Archbishop Peter Comensoli, created a new Melbourne Archdiocese Catholic Schools system, relieving the parish priest of the direct responsibility for parish schools.

The Vietnamese Influence

For a century, Irish Catholicism was dominant in the Australian church. For the first century of the parish of St John the Evangelist, all but two of the 12 parish priests had been born overseas, nine of them in Ireland. But this was to change in the second century of the parish, with only one born in Ireland. Seven were Australian natives, and four born elsewhere.

In 2005, 26-year-old year-old Vinh Nguyen arrived in Australia from Vietnam to study to become a priest for the Archdiocese of Melbourne. Born at Tan Cao-Dien Nguyen, Dien Chau District, Nghe An Province in 1979, the third of nine children, Vinh attended Dien Nguyen's Primary & Secondary and Dien Chau 3 High School before studying to be a teacher at Nghe An Teaching College-Vinh City, Vietnam. He graduated with a Bachelor of Mathematics and became a Math teacher at Dien Truong Secondary School and then at Dien Nguyen Secondary School.

Vinh learned English at the Royal Melbourne Institute of Technology and Australian Catholic University before commencing the seminary program at Corpus Christi College in Carlton Victoria and studied at Catholic Theological College. He graduated from the University of Divinity with a Diploma in Philosophy and Bachelor of Theology and Master of Theology. He was ordained a priest in June 2014 at St Patrick's Cathedral by Archbishop Denis Hart. Before his posting to Heidelberg in June

2022, he served at a number of parishes, including Brunswick, East Brunswick, Sunshine, Doncaster and Yea.

Fr Vinh's immediate task was to reinvigorate a parish severely affected by Covid and the consequences of social isolation. With the support of a vibrant community, parishioners returned to services and other activities. The 2023 census revealed a multi-ethnic congregation, with parishioners from more than 30 countries, including growing numbers from Indo-Pacific nations.

The chaplaincy outreach to the local hospitals was also resumed, including Masses at the Mercy. An Assistant Priest, Fr John Pereira, was appointed to Heidelberg to help with the hospital outreach. Closer engagement with neighbouring parishes, Pius X at Heidelberg West and St Martin of Tours, Rosanna, was also fostered.

Fr Vinh and his Finance Committee also turned attention to the parish property. A minor renovations programme in 2024 included the installation of new, safer steps at the rear entrance to the church, an upgraded foyer, and a new confessional to meet canonical and secular legal requirements.

A statue of St Mary of the Cross was installed in the chapel, which was dedicated by Archbishop Peter Comensoli to one of the Heidelberg Mission's first parishioners, Mary MacKillop.

Plans were also being prepared for the 175th anniversary of the parish and more extensive renovations to the church. The parish began discussions with the Archdiocese about its future needs, including the possible development of the land at 58 Yarra Street, which had been purchased by Fr Sheehy as an investment some five decades earlier.

Benedict XVI and Francis

When the long reign of John Paul II came to an end in 2005, he was replaced by his former confidant, Cardinal Joseph Ratzinger as Benedict XVI. During his eight-year term, Benedict continued the mission of his predecessor, advocating for a return to fundamental Christian values as a counter to growing secularisation in the west.

The election of the Argentinian Archbishop Jorge Bergoglio as Pope Francis in 2013, following the retirement of Benedict XVI, marked a new phase in the universal church.

Towards 2026

As the nation entered the second decade of the 21st century, the age of certainty gave way to an era of anxiety. A Royal Commission into Institutional Responses to Child Sexual Abuse revealed historical abuse by some clergy, findings to which the Catholic Bishops Conference and the Catholic Religious Australia established a

Truth, Justice and Healing Council. The Royal Commission left many Catholics bewildered and perplexed at the historical events. Few had any idea of the harm that had been perpetrated by a relatively small number of clergy and religious, yet the disclosures impacted all.

Stable government was replaced by frequent changes. A mood of introspection was exacerbated by the impact of the Covid 19 pandemic as the lockdown of Victoria — some of the longest and most severe restrictions globally — were enforced. The Indigenous Voice referendum was overwhelmingly rejected by Australians. The Elizabethan age came to an end after seven decades and Charles III became the King of Australia.

As St John the Evangelist approaches its 175th anniversary, Melbourne is on track to become the largest city in Australia, and the Archdiocese the most populous. Whereas the Heidelberg Mission was once the pivot of growth, it is now the new outer suburbs, especially in the north and the west of the metropolitan area.

The Sanctuary and Nave, 2024 (The author).

17

A Mission to Evangelise

The history of the Heidelberg Mission and the parish of St John the Evangelist mirrors the story of the Catholic Church in Australia.

Apart from the first decade of the church in Melbourne when a French and English influence was present, Irish Catholicism has predominated with many of the clergy and members of the episcopacy drawn from the Emerald Island. Of the 12 parish priests in the first century of the Heidelberg parish, nine were born and/or educated in Ireland. It was well into the 20th century before Australian born and educated priests replaced men from Ireland. Apart from Ireland, four of the 23 parish priests were born overseas. At least 13 parishioners have entered the priesthood, with one becoming a bishop, John A Kelly, an auxiliary bishop of Melbourne; and more than 30 joined religious orders.

Secondly, the religious orders have been critical in the establishment and expansion of the Catholic school system. The contribution of the Sisters of Mercy to the education of generations of young people at Heidelberg and surrounding areas is immeasurable; a pattern observed across the nation with many different religious orders. Catherine McAuley could not have imagined the enormous impact that the successors of the three sisters who travelled to Melbourne in 1857 would have on the new colony.

Thirdly, although there were Catholics in Australia from many different countries in the 1800s, the church has become increasingly multiethnic since World War II. A census of Heidelberg parishioners in 2023 revealed a growing number of parishioners who were born overseas, many in Indo-Pacific nations.

The appointment of Fr Vinh Nguyen in 2023 as parish priest reflected the growing influence of the Vietnamese in ranks of the clergy in the decades since large numbers emigrated in the 1980s. The appointment of Bishop Vincent Long OFM Conv — who was born in 1961 in Dong Nai in Vietnam — first as an auxiliary in Melbourne (2011) and subsequently as the Bishop of Parramatta in 2016, mirrored the phenomenon.

Fourthly, the fall in the numbers of marriages and baptisms in the local church exposes the wane in participation and rising secularism in the west, Australia included. Estimated Catholic church attendance fell in Australia from just under a million in 1991 to about 600,000 in 2016. In the Archdiocese of Melbourne, baptisms declined from more than 13,000 in 2013 to less than

10,000 in 2023; while weddings in a church declined from about 2,400 to 1,200. A small counter to this trend in Australia has been the increase in the numbers of adults participating in the RCIA programs in recent years. In many parts of the world Christianity continues to grow and thrive.

Finally, the fall in active church participation has resulted in less young men entering the priesthood — and men and women, the religious orders — and the consolidation of parishes. Some of the parishes that sprung from St John the Evangelist have more recently joined cluster arrangements, a trend that is likely to continue in the years to come.

As this brief history demonstrates, as an institution, the Church has understood that necessary change is a key to its conservation and mission.

Conclusion

Writing in the *Acts of the Apostles*, Luke reminded Christians of their mission to evangelise: "You are to be my witnesses in Jerusalem and throughout Judea, in Samaria, and to the ends of the earth." (Acts 1:8)

For almost two centuries, the priests and parishioners of St John the Evangelist have pursued the mission entrusted to them in 1848, to evangelise the new colony. It was a calling they responded to generously for decade after decade, constructing churches, establishing schools and spreading the Christian gospel. More than 20 churches and parishes were created from the original Heidelberg Mission. For decades, parishioners understood that their work was in the world in which they lived.

The nature of the efforts changed from era to era: at first, it was to build the schools and churches required by a growing population. While this endeavour continued for over a century, other opportunities arose, including the chaplaincy to the hospitals and the provision of other social services. With waning church attendance, the future task may be to evangelise those who have been baptised but are infrequent church attendees — yet enrol their children in Catholic schools.

The Parable of the Talents (Matthew 25: 14-30) reminds Christians that their abilities and skills should not be hidden under a bush. The very essence of Christianity is to love our neighbour. This is not an abstract notion, but involves a real effort to reach out and support those around us. In the words of the St John the Evangelist Parish Prayer, this means especially 'the stranger, the needy, the sick and the lonely.'

The historic and continuing mission of the parish is to evangelise.

Appendix

Parish Priests 1851 – 2025

1851	Viventius Bourgeois
1857	Gerald A Ward
1858	John Hoyne
1862	William M Finn
1879	John Horan
1882	Dennis F O'Callaghan
1907	Patrick M Parker
1915	Michael F McKenna
1922	Thomas Power
1929	James Norris
1944	Patrick Power
1949	Patrick J O'Connor
1960	Bernard Payne
1965	Mortimer FitzGerald
1971	Michael Sheehy
1979	Robert Coghlan
1984	Walter James Atkins
1987	Barry Whelan
1995	Anthony Girolami
2002	Edward Teal
2013	Mario Zammit mssp (Administrator) PP from 2016
2021	Joel Peart
2023	Vinh Nguyen

Select Bibliography

Andrews, Kevin (2016) *Joseph Lyons and the management of adversity* [Redlands Bay, Qld, Connor Court]

Archdiocese of Melbourne, Vicar-General's office, *Marriages and Baptisms*, various years.

Australian Dictionary of Biography (various years and entries) [Canberra, National Centre for Biography, Australian National University]

Blainey, Geoffrey (2003) *A short history of the world* [Chicago, Ivan R Dee]

Cavanough, Maurice (1978) *The Melbourne Cup 1861 – 1982* [South Yarra, Melbourne, Currey O'Neil]

Clark, Jane and Whitelaw, Bridget (1985) *Golden Summer: Heidelberg and Beyond* [Melbourne, International Cultural Corporation of Australia]

Cummins, Cyril, ed (1971) *Heidelberg since 1836 - a pictorial history* [Heidelberg, Heidelberg Historical Society]

Evans, A. G. (2010) *William Wardell: Building with Conviction* [Redlands Bay, Qld, Connor Court]

Fauchery, Antoine (1857) trans. A.R. Chisholm, *Letters from a Miner in Australia* [Melbourne, Georgian House, 1965]

Footprints (various years) [Melbourne, Melbourne Diocesan Historical Commission]

Garden, Donald S (1972) *Heidelberg: the land and its people* [Carlton, Melbourne University Press]

Havel, Václav (1978) (Paul Wilson, ed) *The Power of the Powerless* [Hutchinson, London, 1985]

IBISWorld, *Church attendance in Australia:* https://www.ibisworld.com/au/bed/church-attendance/76/

Johnson, Richard (1792) An address to the inhabitants of the colonies established in New South Wales and Norfolk Island, [London, The Author] iv

Kelly, Paul (1994) *The end of certainty: power, politics and business in Australia* [St Leonards, NSW, Allen & Unwin]

Kelly, Vivienne (2003) *Dixon of Botany Bay: the convict priest from Wexford* [Strathfield, St Paul's]

Marsden, Samuel "A Few Observations on the Toleration of the Catholic Religion in New South Wales", memorandum, cited in Robert Hughes, *A Fatal Shore: A History of the Transportation of Convicts to Australia, 1787-1868.* [Great Britain, Collins Harvill]

McMahon, John (1999-2000) *The early history of the Catholic Church in the Port Phillip District of Victoria, Australia* [Heidelberg, St John the Evangelist]

Moran, Cardinal Patrick (2017) 'Was Australia Discovered by De Quirosin the Year 1606,' first published in 1901. *Connor Court Quarterly*, Volume 12, Spring 2017.

Niall, Brenda, Josephine Dunn and Frances O'Neill (2018) *Newman College: a history 1918-2018* [Parkville, Newman College]

Perkins, Harold (1984) *The convict priests* [Rosanna, Victoria, H. Perkins]

Ross, John, ed (1993) *Chronicle of Australia* [Ringwood, Chronicle Communications]

Slattery, Geoff (ed) (2008) *The Australian Game of Football since*

1858 [Melbourne, Geoff Slattery Publishing for the Australian Football League]

Strong, David (1999) *The Australian Dictionary of Jesuit Biography 1848 – 1998* [Rushcutters Bay, NSW, Halstead Press]

Synan, Peter (2014) *Strive after better things: St Patrick's College, Sale: a history* [Sale, St Patrick's Old Collegians Association]

Vaughan, Eileen (1982) *St John's on the Hill* [Heidelberg, The Parish of St John the Evangelist]

Victorian Places (2015) [Melbourne and Brisbane, Monash University and the University of Queensland]

Milton Keynes UK
Ingram Content Group UK Ltd.
UKHW022137291124
451915UK00011B/733